Second Edition

GREAT JOBS

FOR

Anthropology Majors

VGM CAREER BOOKS

New York   Chicago   San Francisco   Lisbon   London   Madrid   Mexico City
Milan   New Delhi   San Juan   Seoul   Singapore   Sydney   Toronto

Library of Congress Cataloging-in-Publication Data

Camenson, Blythe.
    Great jobs for anthropology majors / Blythe Camenson. — 2nd ed.
        p.   cm.
    Includes index.
    ISBN 0-07-143733-9 (alk. paper)
      1. Anthropology—Vocational guidance.   I. Title.
  GN41.8.C35   2004
  301'.023—dc22   2004002956

2 3 4 5 6 7 8 9 0 DOC/DOC   9 8 7

ISBN 0-07-143733-9

McGraw-Hill books are available at special quantity discounts to use as premiums and sales promotions, or for use in corporate training programs. For more information, please write to the Director of Special Sales, Professional Publishing, McGraw-Hill, Two Penn Plaza, New York, NY 10121-2298. Or contact your local bookstore.

This book is printed on acid-free paper.

Contents

Acknowledgments

The author would like to thank the following professionals for providing information and advice on careers in anthropology.

Nadine Bendycki, Founder and Principal Consultant, MarketWhys, Cleveland, Ohio

Tiffanie Bourassa, Archeological Technician and Administrative Clerk, Southeast Archeological Center, National Park Service, Tallahassee, Florida

Gordon Bronitsky, Consultant and President, Bronitsky and Associates, Albuquerque, New Mexico

Bryan Byrne, Design Anthropologist, Alameda, California

David Carlson, Associate Professor of Anthropology, Texas A&M University, College Station, Texas

James Dow, Professor, Department of Anthropology, Oakland University, Rochester, Michigan

Gregory Finnegan, Associate Librarian for Public Services and Head of Reference, Tozzer Library, Harvard University, Cambridge, Massachusetts

Joan Gardner, Former Chief Conservator, Carnegie Museum of Natural History, Pittsburgh, Pennsylvania

Sharon Hodges, Organizational Anthropologist, Department of Child and Family Studies, Louis de la Parte Florida Mental Health Institute, University of South Florida, Tampa, Florida

Cris Johnsrud, Consultant, Pathfinder Research, Gainesville, Florida

Jim King, Former Director, Carnegie Museum of Natural History, Pittsburgh, Pennsylvania

Kristin Kuckelman, Senior Research Archaeologist, Crow Canyon
   Archaeological Center, Cortez, Colorado
Richard Meindl, Professor and Chairperson, Department of
   Anthropology, Kent State University, Kent, Ohio
Sharlotte Neely, Professor and Coordinator of Anthropology, Northern
   Kentucky University, Highland Heights, Kentucky
Reed Riner, Professor of Anthropology, Northern Arizona University,
   Flagstaff, Arizona

Introduction

Anthropology: Charting Your Future

Success is not the key to happiness. Happiness is the key to success.
If you love what you are doing, you will be successful.
—ALBERT SCHWEITZER

You may have heard this before (most likely from engineering majors or students in some other technical field): "Oh, anthropology. You'll certainly be well educated—but unemployed."

Or how about this: "There's absolutely nothing you can do with a B.A. in anthropology."

Like many students, you might be progressing through your anthropology program, taking required courses and signing up for electives, but not really sure where you'll be on graduation day, never mind five or ten years from now.

Maybe some not-so-savvy friends or family members have advised: "If you want to have a career, you need to be in some sort of professional program. Nursing. Engineering. Accounting. Anything but anthropology."

And you worry that they're right. But those professional programs aren't for you. Those fields don't interest you.

So, what in the world *are* you going to do with that B.A. or B.S. in anthropology? Are you headed toward a dead end? Will you graduate with nothing more than the ability to talk to people at a cocktail party about a variety of interesting and socially relevant topics? One thing is sure: intelligent conversation does not pay the bills.

It's time to put all those fears aside. With some planning and knowledge of your options, you will find that your career choices are as diverse as the number of anthropology majors.

Walking into a job with a bachelor's degree might not be as hard as you—or your friends and family—think. You just have to be creative and imaginative.

Anthropology is a broad field. Employment possibilities are similarly broad, and some areas of anthropology have better job prospects than others. As with any field, the more education, training, and experience you have, the better your chances of finding a job you like.

The Skills You'll Acquire

In addition to a diverse knowledge base specific to the field—for example, ethnographic methods, archaeological excavation, or the characteristics of specific cultures—undergraduates in anthropology acquire a wide range of skills. These skills can be applied in many different fields, such as business, research, teaching, and public service. The skills and experience you will acquire include:

- Oral and written communication
- Interviewing
- Observation
- Formulating and testing hypotheses
- Conducting and explaining scientific research
- Writing descriptive reports and analytical papers
- Critical thinking skills that take an integrated, holistic approach to social and organizational systems
- Analyzing the root causes of social problems
- Cross-cultural, interethnic, and international communication
- Working cooperatively with people from a wide variety of cultural backgrounds
- Foreign language skills
- Analytical reading
- Operating and using information from computers, especially in statistics and database management
- Careful record keeping
- Attention to details
- Social ease in foreign cultures

One of the most important ways to develop applied skills is through practical experience gained from internships and volunteer work. Ways to find and benefit from these experiences are covered in Part Two of this book.

Possible Job Settings

The skills just listed open doors in many directly and indirectly related employment settings. Holders of bachelor's degrees in anthropology find work in museums and zoos and similar public education institutions; social service agencies, both governmental and private; ethnic, cultural, and immigrant organizations; elementary and secondary schools; health-care agencies that serve diverse populations; foreign service and foreign aid agencies; international businesses; advertising firms; market development companies; cultural resource management firms; educational research agencies; economic development agencies; forensic analysis agencies; and more. Completing a master's degree or a doctorate will open even more doors or allow you in the same doors at a higher level of responsibility and compensation.

Dozens of job settings and career possibilities are covered in Part Two.

Strategies for Improving Your Odds

A number of approaches will improve your chances for employment:

1. Choose a double major to give yourself more skills and training that an employer would be looking for. Good choices to combine with anthropology are math, history, biology, social work, environmental sciences, or computer science.
2. Be creative. Design your own interdisciplinary degree with an eye to a particular field or to starting your own business.
3. Learn one or more additional languages. Reasonable competency or, better yet, fluency in another language can open more doors for you.
4. Become computer proficient. At the very least, master a word processing and database management program. Become familiar with statistics and learn a computer program to work with them. Become proficient at researching on the Internet and learn how to find information that would help your employer.
5. Enhance your résumé while still in school. Get as much experience as you can, by volunteering or through paid or unpaid internships. Offer to help faculty members with their research projects. Volunteer your time at museums or relevant professional associations. Your work will result in recommendations for graduate school or future employment.

6. Seriously consider going on to graduate school. Most good jobs in anthropology require at least a master's degree, but a Ph.D. is mandatory if you want to teach or do research at the university level.

Advice from a Professional

Dr. Sharlotte Neely, Professor of Anthropology at Northern Kentucky University, has this to say:

"I love being an anthropologist. At times, it offers all the excitement of an Indiana Jones story and all the challenge of a Tony Hillerman mystery. I will never forget riding horses in Canyon de Chelly with a Navajo guide in search of Anasazi ruins or living in a remote, haunted cabin on the Cherokee reservation. I have danced around a campfire, my face painted with magical designs, and I have slept under the stars. I have climbed inside the Great Pyramid in Egypt and stood atop the Pyramid of the Moon in Mexico. As an applied cultural anthropologist, I have researched and written a report that stopped a highway from barreling through an Indian reservation. And every time I do something like that, I marvel that I actually get paid to be an anthropologist.

"If I were to win the lottery tomorrow and never had to work another day in my life, I would not quit my job, because the money is only one of the reasons I am an anthropologist.

"But you should also know that I enjoy the more contemplative tasks that go into being an anthropologist, too, at least as I define anthropology. I enjoy teaching, even topics such as kinship terminology, and watching the faces of my students as they 'get it' for the first time. I enjoy analyzing my research and the thrill that comes when I 'get it' for the first time. I enjoy writing books and articles about the people I have studied and realizing that long after I am dead, someone will pull a dusty book I have written from a library shelf—or punch it up on the Internet—and feel some of the same wonder I did so long ago.

"How will you make a living out of something that gives you satisfaction? Some areas of anthropology are more popular than others. Most of us, often as children, have read the story of archaeologist Howard Carter as he gazed upon the treasures of King Tut's tomb for the first time. Archaeology is a subfield of anthropology. Forensic anthropology is another popular subfield, and I realized recently just how popular when I ran across a children's book, *The Bone Detectives: How Forensic Anthropologists Solve Crimes and*

Uncover Mysteries of the Dead. Archaeology and forensic anthropology both seem like such interesting ways of making a living. Is that possible? The answer is yes and no.

"For archaeology, the answer is a loud yes. There are more than half a dozen contract archaeology companies operating in my area and hiring people at every college-degree level from the bachelor's to the doctorate. Throw in local universities and museums that hire archaeologists, and the job market is even bigger. And that is true of archaeology all over the world. So, if your interest is archaeology, go for it.

"What about forensic anthropology? Exciting? Yes. Jobs that pay money? Only for the lucky few. There are only about 150 forensic anthropologists in the United States, and only about 15 of them work full-time as forensic anthropologists. The rest of them do forensic anthropology part-time and support themselves working in related areas of anthropology, biology, or medicine. Part-timers might get only one or two grisly cases a year. If your interest is forensic anthropology, you need to decide how the availability of work affects your career choice. Could you be happy earning your living in a related area of anthropology in which there are numerous jobs and doing forensics here and there?

"Other job prospects in anthropology lie somewhere along the continuum between archaeology and forensic anthropology. Applied anthropology and environmental studies lie closer to archaeology along the job continuum. College teaching has slipped toward the forensic anthropology end of the continuum when it comes to new jobs as a professor (although that may be changing for the better). Could you be happy teaching in college part-time and making your living as a contract archaeologist or an applied researcher?

"What should your strategy be in your quest for a career in anthropology? That is something for you to decide. But I can tell you what I would do, with what I know now, if I were just starting out:

"I would have a two-pronged approach. I would prepare myself to go after the career in anthropology that I most wanted, job availability or not. When it comes to career, I am willing to be a risk taker. But even risk takers hedge their bets. The second part of my approach would be to amass as many job skills as possible in every area of anthropology and related fields, especially the areas in which jobs are more readily available.

"Follow your heart, but in a pragmatic sort of way. Take courses that will develop important skills: anthropology courses such as ethnographic methods, museum methods, laboratory methods, and archaeology field school, and courses outside of anthropology such as statistics, a foreign language, computer skills, historical research, photography, and sociological methods.

"And accumulate work experience, even if at first you have to do it on a volunteer basis, with museums, contract archaeology companies, and human services organizations."

The Road Ahead

In Part One of this book, you will learn many valuable tips on the job search, especially how to prepare yourself and make a case for the ideal job you are seeking.

In Part Two, you will explore a variety of career paths. Some are open to any anthropology major; some are more defined and require training in specific subfields, and some require further education or training—master's degrees and doctorates. Chapter 5 will give you a broad overview of the various paths and the training and preparation you'll need for them. The remaining chapters will help you narrow those paths.

Once you've found the path you want to follow, you'll realize how important your anthropology degree is in reaching your ultimate destination.

PART ONE

THE JOB SEARCH

The Self-Assessment

Self-assessment is the process by which you begin to acknowledge your own particular blend of education, experiences, values, needs, and goals. It provides the foundation for career planning and the entire job search process. Self-assessment involves looking inward and asking yourself what can sometimes prove to be difficult questions. This self-examination should lead to an intimate understanding of your personal traits, your personal values, your consumption patterns and economic needs, your longer-term goals, your skill base, your preferred skills, and your underdeveloped skills.

You come to the self-assessment process knowing yourself well in some of these areas, but you may still be uncertain about other aspects. You may be well aware of your consumption patterns, but have you spent much time specifically identifying your longer-term goals or your personal values as they relate to work? No matter what level of self-assessment you have undertaken to date, it is now time to clarify all of these issues and questions as they relate to the job search.

The knowledge you gain in the self-assessment process will guide the rest of your job search. In this book, you will learn about all of the following tasks:

- Writing résumés and cover letters
- Researching careers and networking
- Interviewing and job offer considerations

In each of these steps, you will rely on and often return to the understanding gained through your self-assessment. Any individual seeking employment must be able and willing to express these facets of his or her personality to recruiters and interviewers throughout the job search. This communication allows you to show the world who you are so that together with employers you can determine whether there will be a workable match with a given job or career path.

How to Conduct a Self-Assessment

The self-assessment process goes on naturally all the time. People ask you to clarify what you mean, you make a purchasing decision, or you begin a new relationship. You react to the world and the world reacts to you. How you understand these interactions and any changes you might make because of them are part of the natural process of self-discovery. There is, however, a more comprehensive and efficient way to approach self-assessment with regard to employment.

Because self-assessment can become a complex exercise, we have distilled it into a seven-step process that provides an effective basis for undertaking a job search. The seven steps include the following:

1. Understanding your personal traits
2. Identifying your personal values
3. Calculating your economic needs
4. Exploring your longer-term goals
5. Enumerating your skill base
6. Recognizing your preferred skills
7. Assessing skills needing further development

As you work through your self-assessment, you might want to create a worksheet similar to the one shown in Exhibit 1.1, starting on the following page. Or you might want to keep a journal of the thoughts you have as you undergo this process. There will be many opportunities to revise your self-assessment as you start down the path of seeking a career.

Step 1 Understand Your Personal Traits

Each person has a unique personality that he or she brings to the job search process. Gaining a better understanding of your personal traits can help you evaluate job and career choices. Identifying these traits and then finding employment that allows you to draw on at least some of them can create a rewarding and fulfilling work experience. If potential employment doesn't allow you to use these preferred traits, it is important to decide whether you can find other ways to express them or whether you would be better off not

Exhibit 1.1
SELF-ASSESSMENT WORKSHEET

Step 1. Understand Your Personal Traits
    The personal traits that describe me are:
    (Include all of the words that describe you.)
    The ten personal traits that most accurately describe me are:
    (List these ten traits.)

Step 2. Identify Your Personal Values
    Working conditions that are important to me include:
    (List working conditions that would have to exist for you to accept a position.)
    The values that go along with my working conditions are:
    (Write down the values that correspond to each working condition.)
    Some additional values I've decided to include are:
    (List those values you identify as you conduct this job search.)

Step 3. Calculate Your Economic Needs
    My estimated minimum annual salary requirement is:
    (Write the salary you have calculated based on your budget.)
    Starting salaries for the positions I'm considering are:
    (List the name of each job you are considering and the associated starting salary.)

Step 4. Explore Your Longer-Term Goals
    My thoughts on longer-term goals right now are:
    (Jot down some of your longer-term goals as you know them right now.)

Step 5. Enumerate Your Skill Base
    The general skills I possess are:
    (List the skills that underlie tasks you are able to complete.)
    The specific skills I possess are:
    (List more technical or specific skills that you possess, and indicate your level of expertise.)
    General and specific skills that I want to promote to employers for the jobs I'm considering are:
    (List general and specific skills for each type of job you are considering.)

continued

Step 6. Recognize Your Preferred Skills

Skills that I would like to use on the job include:

(List skills that you hope to use on the job, and indicate how often you'd like to use them.)

Step 7. Assess Skills Needing Further Development

Some skills that I'll need to acquire for the jobs I'm considering include:

(Write down skills listed in job advertisements or job descriptions that you don't currently possess.)

I believe I can build these skills by:

(Describe how you plan to acquire these skills.)

considering this type of job. Interests and hobbies pursued outside of work hours can be one way to use personal traits you don't have an opportunity to draw on in your work. For example, if you consider yourself an outgoing person and the kinds of jobs you are examining allow little contact with other people, you may be able to achieve the level of interaction that is comfortable for you outside of your work setting. If such a compromise seems impractical or otherwise unsatisfactory, you probably should explore only jobs that provide the interaction you want and need on the job.

Many young adults who are not very confident about their employability will downplay their need for income. They will say, "Money is not all that important if I love my work." But if you begin to document exactly what you need for housing, transportation, insurance, clothing, food, and utilities, you will begin to understand that some jobs cannot meet your financial needs and it doesn't matter how wonderful the job is. If you have to worry each payday about bills and other financial obligations, you won't be very effective on the job. Begin now to be honest with yourself about your needs.

Begin the self-assessment process by creating an inventory of your personal traits. Make a list of as many words as possible to describe yourself. Words like *accurate, creative, future-oriented, relaxed,* or *structured* are just a few examples. In addition, you might ask people who know you well how they might describe you.

Focus on Selected Personal Traits. Of all the traits you identified, select the ten you believe most accurately describe you. Keep track of these ten traits.

Consider Your Personal Traits in the Job Search Process. As you begin exploring jobs and careers, watch for matches between your personal traits and the job descriptions you read. Some jobs will require many personal traits you know you possess, and others will not seem to match those traits.

A researcher's work, for example, requires self-discipline, motivation, curiosity, and observation. Researchers often work alone, with limited opportunities to interact with others. Professors, on the other hand, must interact regularly with students and colleagues to carry out the teaching program. Educators need strong interpersonal and verbal skills, imagination, and a good sense of humor. They must enjoy being in front of groups and must become skilled at presenting information using a wide variety of methods.

Your ability to respond to changing conditions, your decision-making ability, productivity, creativity, and verbal skills all have a bearing on your success in and enjoyment of your work life. To better guarantee success, be sure to take the time needed to understand these traits in yourself.

Step 2   Identify Your Personal Values

Your personal values affect every aspect of your life, including employment, and they develop and change as you move through life. Values can be defined as principles that we hold in high regard, qualities that are important and desirable to us. Some values aren't ordinarily connected to work (love, beauty, color, light, relationships, family, or religion), and others are (autonomy, cooperation, effectiveness, achievement, knowledge, and security). Our values determine, in part, the level of satisfaction we feel in a particular job.

Define Acceptable Working Conditions. One facet of employment is the set of working conditions that must exist for someone to consider taking a job.

Each of us would probably create a unique list of acceptable working conditions, but items that might be included on many people's lists are the amount of money you would need to be paid, how far you are willing to drive or travel, the amount of freedom you want in determining your own schedule, whether you would be working with people or data or things, and the types of tasks you would be willing to do. Your conditions might include statements of working conditions you will *not* accept; for example, you might not be willing to work at night or on weekends or holidays.

If you were offered a job tomorrow, what conditions would have to exist for you to realistically consider accepting the position? Take some time and make a list of these conditions.

Realize Associated Values. Your list of working conditions can be used to create an inventory of your values relating to jobs and careers you are exploring. For example, if one of your conditions stated that you wanted to earn at least $30,000 per year, the associated value would be financial gain. If another condition was that you wanted to work with a friendly group of people, the value that went along with that might be belonging or interaction with people.

Relate Your Values to the World of Work. As you read the job descriptions you come across either in this book, in newspapers and magazines, or online, think about the values associated with each position.

For example, a curator in a natural history museum is responsible for the preservation of the collection and for implementing its accessibility to the public. Associated values are precision, effectiveness, and community.

At least some of the associated values in the field you're exploring should match those you extracted from your list of working conditions. Take a second look at any values that don't match up. How important are they to you? What will happen if they are not satisfied on the job? Can you incorporate those personal values elsewhere? Your answers need to be brutally honest. As you continue your exploration, be sure to add to your list any additional values that occur to you.

Step 3   Calculate Your Economic Needs

Each of us grew up in an environment that provided for certain basic needs, such as food and shelter, and, to varying degrees, other needs that we now consider basic, such as cable television, e-mail, or an automobile. Needs such as privacy, space, and quiet, which at first glance may not appear to be monetary needs, may add to housing expenses and so should be considered as you examine your economic needs. For example, if you place a high value on a large, open living space for yourself, it would be difficult to satisfy that need without an associated high housing cost, especially in a densely populated city environment.

As you prepare to move into the world of work and become responsible for meeting your own basic needs, it is important to consider the salary you will need to be able to afford a satisfying standard of living. The three-step process outlined here will help you plan a budget, which in turn will allow you to evaluate the various career choices and geographic locations you are considering. The steps include (1) developing a realistic budget, (2) examining starting salaries, and (3) using a cost-of-living index.

Develop a Realistic Budget. Each of us has certain expectations for the kind of lifestyle we want to maintain. To begin the process of defining your economic needs, it will be helpful to determine what you expect to spend on routine monthly expenses. These expenses include housing, food, transportation, entertainment, utilities, loan repayments, and revolving charge accounts. You may not currently spend anything for certain items, but you probably will have to once you begin supporting yourself. As you develop this budget, be generous in your estimates, but keep in mind any items that could be reduced or eliminated. If you are not sure about the cost of a certain item, talk with family or friends who would be able to give you a realistic estimate.

If this is new or difficult for you, start to keep a log of expenses right now. You may be surprised at how much you actually spend each month for food or stamps or magazines. Household expenses and personal grooming items can often loom very large in a budget, as can auto repairs or home maintenance.

Income taxes must also be taken into consideration when examining salary requirements. State and local taxes vary, so it is difficult to calculate exactly the effect of taxes on the amount of income you need to generate. To roughly estimate the gross income necessary to generate your minimum annual salary requirement, multiply the minimum salary you have calculated by a factor of 1.35. The resulting figure will be an approximation of what your gross income would need to be, given your estimated expenses.

Examine Starting Salaries. Starting salaries for each of the career tracks are provided throughout this book. These salary figures can be used in conjunction with the cost-of-living index (discussed in the next section) to determine whether you would be able to meet your basic economic needs in a given geographic location.

Use a Cost-of-Living Index. If you are thinking about trying to get a job in a geographic region other than the one where you now live, understanding differences in the cost of living will help you come to a more informed decision about making a move. By using a cost-of-living index, you can compare salaries offered and the cost of living in different locations with what you know about the salaries offered and the cost of living in your present location.

Many variables are used to calculate the cost-of-living index. Often included are housing, groceries, utilities, transportation, health care, clothing, and entertainment expenses. Right now you do not need to worry about the details associated with calculating a given index. The main purpose of this exercise is to help you understand that pay ranges for entry-level positions may not vary greatly, but the cost of living in different locations *can* vary tremendously.

Suppose you were interested in working as an assistant registrar for a small museum. If you lived in Cleveland, Ohio, for example, you would earn, on average, $26,000 annually. But let's say you're also thinking about moving to New York, Los Angeles, or Denver. You know you can live on $26,000 in Cleveland, but you want to be able to equate that salary in other locations you're considering. How much will you need to earn in those locations to do this? Figuring the cost of living for each city will show you.

In any cost-of-living index, the number 100 represents the national average. Each city is assigned an index number based on current prices in that city for items included in the index, such as housing and food. In the index used for the table that follows, New York was assigned the number 213.3, Los Angeles's index was 124.6, Denver's was 100.0, and Cleveland's index was 114.3. In other words, it costs more than twice as much to live in New York as it does in Denver.

To determine the equivalent salary in each location, first divide the index of the city you are considering by the index of the city you are in. Then multiply the result by the salary. You can set up a table to determine exactly how much you would have to earn in each of these cities to have the same buying power that you have in Cleveland.

JOB: ASSISTANT REGISTRAR

City	Index	Equivalent Salary
New York	213.3	
		× $26,000 = $48,520 in New York
Cleveland	114.3	
Los Angeles	124.6	
		× $26,000 = $28,343 in Los Angeles
Cleveland	114.3	
Denver	100.0	
		× $26,000 = $22,747 in Denver
Cleveland	114.3	

You would have to earn $48,519 in New York, $28,342 in Los Angeles, and $22,747 in Denver to match the buying power of $26,000 in Cleveland. If you would like to determine whether it's financially worthwhile to make any of these moves, one more piece of information is needed: the salaries of assistant registrars in these other cities.

If you moved to New York and secured employment as an assistant registrar in a museum at the same salary, you would not be able to maintain a lifestyle similar to the one you led in Cleveland; in fact, you would have to add more than 100 percent to your income to maintain a similar lifestyle in New York. On the other hand, if you took the job with the same salary in Denver, you would increase your buying power given the cost of living there.

You can work through a similar exercise for any type of job you are considering and for many locations when current salary information is available. It will be worth your time to undertake this analysis if you are seriously considering a relocation. By doing so you will be able to make an informed choice.

Step 4 Explore Your Longer-Term Goals

There is no question that when we first begin working, our goals are to use our skills and education in a job that will reward us with employment, income, and status relative to the preparation we brought with us to this position. If we are not being paid as much as we feel we should for our level of education or if job demands don't provide the intellectual stimulation we had hoped for, we experience unhappiness and as a result often seek other employment.

Most jobs we consider "good" are those that fulfill our basic "lower-level" needs of security, food, clothing, shelter, income, and productive work. But even when our basic needs are met and our jobs are secure and productive, we as individuals are constantly changing. As we change, the demands and expectations we place on our jobs may change. Fortunately, some jobs grow and change with us, and this explains why some people are happy throughout many years in a job.

But more often people are bigger than the jobs they fill. We have more goals and needs than any job could satisfy. These are "higher-level" needs of self-esteem, companionship, affection, and an increasing desire to feel we are employing ourselves in the most effective way possible. Not all of these higher-level needs can be met through employment, but for as long as we are employed, we increasingly demand that our jobs play their part in moving us along the path to fulfillment.

Another obvious but important fact is that we change as we mature. Although our jobs also have the potential for change, they may not change as frequently or as markedly as we do. There are increasingly fewer one-job, one-employer careers; we must think about a work future that may involve voluntary or forced moves from employer to employer. Because of that very real possibility, we need to take advantage of the opportunities in each position we hold. Acquiring the skills and competencies associated with each position will keep us viable and attractive as employees. This is particularly true in a job market that not only is technology/computer dependent, but also is populated with more and more small, self-transforming organizations rather than the large, seemingly stable organizations of the past.

A person considering a position as an objects curator in a museum would gain a better perspective on this career by talking to an entry-level conservation technician, a more experienced assistant or associate curator, and finally a director or department head who has had a considerable work history in the curatorial field. Each will have a different perspective, unique concerns, and an individual set of value priorities.

Step 5   Enumerate Your Skill Base

In terms of the job search, skills can be thought of as capabilities that can be developed in school, at work, or by volunteering and then used in specific job settings. Many studies have documented the kinds of skills that employers seek in entry-level applicants. For example, some of the most desired skills for individuals interested in the teaching profession are the ability to interact effectively with students one-on-one, to manage a classroom, to adapt to varying situations as necessary, and to get involved in school activities. Business employers have also identified important qualities, including enthusiasm for the employer's product or service, a businesslike mind, the ability to follow written or oral instructions, the ability to demonstrate self-control, the confidence to suggest new ideas, the ability to communicate with all members of a group, an awareness of cultural differences, and loyalty, to name just a few. You will find that many of these skills are also in the repertoire of qualities demanded in your college major.

To be successful in obtaining any given job, you must be able to demonstrate that you possess a certain mix of skills that will allow you to carry out the duties required by that job. This skill mix will vary a great deal from job to job; to determine the skills necessary for the jobs you are seeking, you can read job advertisements or more generic job descriptions, such as those found later in this book. If you want to be effective in the job search, you must directly show employers that you possess the skills needed to be successful in filling the position. These skills will initially be described on your résumé and then discussed again during the interview process.

Skills are either general or specific. To develop a list of skills relevant to employers, you must first identify the general skills you possess, then list specific skills you have to offer, and, finally, examine which of these skills employers are seeking.

Identify Your General Skills.   Because you possess or will possess a college degree, employers will assume that you can read and write, perform certain basic computations, think critically, and communicate effectively. Employers will want to see that you have acquired these skills, and they will want to know which additional general skills you possess.

One way to begin identifying skills is to write an experiential diary. An experiential diary lists all the tasks you were responsible for completing for each job you've held and then outlines the skills required to do those tasks. You may list several skills for any given task. This diary allows you to distinguish between the tasks you performed and the underlying skills required to complete those tasks. Here's an example:

Tasks	Skills
Answering telephone	Effective use of language, clear diction, ability to direct inquiries, ability to solve problems
Waiting on tables	Poise under conditions of time and pressure, speed, accuracy, good memory, simultaneous completion of tasks, sales skills

For each job or experience you have participated in, develop a worksheet based on the example shown here. On a résumé, you may want to describe these skills rather than simply listing tasks. Skills are easier for the employer to appreciate, especially when your experience is very different from the employment you are seeking. In addition to helping you identify general skills, this experiential diary will prepare you to speak more effectively in an interview about the qualifications you possess.

Identify Your Specific Skills. It may be easier to identify your specific skills because you can definitely say whether you can speak other languages, program a computer, draft a map or diagram, or edit a document using appropriate symbols and terminology.

Using your experiential diary, identify the points in your history where you learned how to do something very specific, and decide whether you have a beginning, intermediate, or advanced knowledge of how to use that particular skill. Right now, be sure to list *every* specific skill you have, and don't consider whether you like using the skill. Write down a list of specific skills you have acquired and the level of competence you possess—beginning, intermediate, or advanced.

Relate Your Skills to Employers. You probably have thought about a couple of different jobs you might be interested in obtaining, and one way to begin relating the general and specific skills you possess to a potential employer's needs is to read actual advertisements for these types of positions (see Part Two for resources listing actual job openings).

For example, you might be interested in a career as a museum educator. A typical job listing might read, "Requires two to five years' experience, organizational and interpersonal skills, imagination, drive, and the ability to work under pressure." If you then used any one of a number of general sources of information that describes the job of museum educator, you would find additional information. Museum educators also develop marketing plans, must be able to translate important concepts into understandable language, write and edit promotional material, and work with artists and other museum staff.

Begin building a comprehensive list of required skills with the first job description you find. Exploring advertisements for and descriptions of several types of related positions will reveal an important core of skills necessary for obtaining the work you're interested in. In building this list, include both general and specific skills.

Following is a sample list of skills needed to be successful as a museum educator. These items were extracted from general resources and actual job listings.

On a separate sheet of paper, try to generate a comprehensive list of required skills for at least one job you are considering.

JOB: MUSEUM EDUCATOR

General Skills

Gather information

Disseminate information

Demonstrate a specific
  body of knowledge

Work in a hectic
  environment

Present a certain image

Meet deadlines

Work well with other people

Think creatively

Possess drive

Be organized

Supervise the work of
  others

Have excellent written
  and verbal skills

Specific Skills

Write PR material

Select illustrations

Write letters

Write memos

Project a professional
  phone presence

Develop marketing plans

Arrange exhibits

Display artwork

Schedule lectures

Evaluate performance

Develop lesson plans

The list of general skills that you develop for a given career path will be valuable for any number of jobs for which you might apply. Many of the specific skills will also be transferable to other types of positions. For example, translating research into language that the public understands, which is a required skill for museum educators, is also a required skill for professors working in a university.

Step 6   Recognize Your Preferred Skills

In the previous section you developed a comprehensive list of skills that relate to particular career paths that are of interest to you. You can now relate these to skills that you prefer to use. We all use a wide range of skills (some researchers say individuals have a repertoire of about five hundred skills), but we may not particularly be interested in using all of them in our work. There may be some skills that come to us more naturally or that we use successfully time and time again and that we want to continue to use; these are best described as our preferred skills. For this exercise use the list of skills that you created for the previous section, and decide which of them you are *most interested in using* in future work and how often you would like to use them. You might be interested in using some skills only occasionally, while others you would like to use more regularly. You probably also have skills that you hope you can use constantly.

As you examine job announcements, look for matches between this list of preferred skills and the qualifications described in the advertisements. These skills should be highlighted on your résumé and discussed in job interviews.

Step 7   Assess Skills Needing Further Development

Previously you compiled a list of general and specific skills required for given positions. You already possess some of these skills; those that remain to be developed are your underdeveloped skills.

If you are just beginning the job search, there may be gaps between the qualifications required for some of the jobs you're considering and the skills you possess. The thought of having to admit to and talk about these underdeveloped skills, especially in a job interview, is a frightening one. One way to put a healthy perspective on this subject is to target and relate your exploration of underdeveloped skills to the types of positions you are seeking. Recognizing these shortcomings and planning to overcome them with either on-the-job training or additional formal education can be a positive way to address the concept of underdeveloped skills.

On your worksheet or in your journal, make a list of up to five general or specific skills required for the positions you're interested in that you *don't currently possess*. For each item list an idea you have for specific action you could take to acquire that skill. Do some brainstorming to come up with possible actions. If you have a hard time generating ideas, talk to people currently working in this type of position, professionals in your college career services office, trusted friends, family members, or members of related professional associations.

In the chapter on interviewing, we will discuss in detail how to effectively address questions about underdeveloped skills. Generally speaking, though, employers want genuine answers to these types of questions. They want you to reveal "the real you," and they also want to see how you answer difficult questions. In taking the positive, targeted approach discussed previously, you show the employer that you are willing to continue to learn and that you have a plan for strengthening your job qualifications.

Use Your Self-Assessment

Exploring entry-level career options can be an exciting experience if you have good resources available and will take the time to use them. Can you effectively complete the following tasks?

1. Understand your personality traits and relate them to career choices
2. Define your personal values
3. Determine your economic needs
4. Explore longer-term goals
5. Understand your skill base
6. Recognize your preferred skills
7. Express a willingness to improve on your underdeveloped skills

If so, then you can more meaningfully participate in the job search process by writing a more effective résumé, finding job titles that represent work you are interested in doing, locating job sites that will provide the opportunity for you to use your strengths and skills, networking in an informed way, participating in focused interviews, getting the most out of follow-up contacts, and evaluating job offers to find those that create a good match between you and the employer. The remaining chapters in Part One guide you through these next steps in the job search process. For many job seekers, this process can take anywhere from three months to a year to implement. The time you will need to put into your job search will depend on the type of job you want and the geographic location where you'd like to work. Think of your effort as a job in itself, requiring you to set aside time each week to complete the needed work. Carefully undertaken efforts may reduce the time you need for your job search.

2

The Résumé and Cover Letter

The task of writing a résumé may seem overwhelming if you are unfamiliar with this type of document, but there are some easily understood techniques that can and should be used. This section was written to help you understand the purpose of the résumé, the different types of résumé formats available, and how to write the sections of information traditionally found on a résumé. We will present examples and explanations that address questions frequently posed by people writing their first résumé or updating an old résumé.

Even within the formats and suggestions given, however, there are infinite variations. True, most résumés follow one of the outlines suggested, but you should feel free to adjust the résumé to suit your needs and make it expressive of your life and experience.

Why Write a Résumé?

The purpose of a résumé is to convince an employer that you should be interviewed. Whether you're mailing, faxing, or e-mailing this document, you'll want to present enough information to show that you can make an immediate and valuable contribution to an organization. A résumé is not an in-depth historical or legal document; later in the job search process you may be asked to document your entire work history on an application form and attest to its validity. The résumé should, instead, highlight relevant information pertaining directly to the organization that will receive the document or to the type of position you are seeking.

We will discuss the chronological and digital résumés in detail here. Functional and targeted résumés, which are used much less often, are briefly discussed. The reasons for using one type of résumé over another and the typical format for each are addressed in the following sections.

The Chronological Résumé

The chronological résumé is the most common of the various résumé formats and therefore the format that employers are most used to receiving. This type of résumé is easy to read and understand because it details the chronological progression of jobs you have held. (See Exhibit 2.1.) It begins with your most recent employment and works back in time. If you have a solid work history or have experience that provided growth and development in your duties and responsibilities, a chronological résumé will highlight these achievements. The typical elements of a chronological résumé include the heading, a career objective, educational background, employment experience, activities, and references.

The Heading
The heading consists of your name, address, telephone number, and other means of contact. This may include a fax number, e-mail address, and your home-page address. If you are using a shared e-mail account or a parent's business fax, be sure to let others who use these systems know that you may receive important professional correspondence via these systems. You wouldn't want to miss a vital e-mail or fax! Likewise, if your résumé directs readers to a personal home page on the Web, be certain it's a professional personal home page designed to be viewed and appreciated by a prospective employer. This may mean making substantial changes in the home page you currently mount on the Web.

The Objective
Without a doubt the objective statement is the most challenging part of the résumé for most writers. Even for individuals who have decided on a career path, it can be difficult to encapsulate all they want to say in one or two brief sentences. For job seekers who are unfocused or unclear about their intentions, trying to write this section can inhibit the entire résumé writing process.

Keep the objective as short as possible and no longer than two short sentences.

Exhibit 2.1
CHRONOLOGICAL RÉSUMÉ

JOHN RUBIN

Duke Hall #133   3229 Church St.
University of New Mexico   Arlington, VA 22432
Albuquerque, NM 87110   (703) 555-8841
(505) 555-7500
(until May 2004)

OBJECTIVE
A career as a field archaeologist. Special interest in historical archaeology.

EDUCATION
Bachelor of Arts in Anthropology
University of New Mexico
May 2004
Overall GPA 3.2 on a 4.0 scale

RELATED COURSES
American Studies   Drafting
Folklore   Surveying
Historic Preservation   Computer-Aided Design

EXPERIENCE
Internship
Albuquerque History Museum
Academic year 2003 to 2004
Worked with a team of archaeologists and anthropologists in the education
    department preparing research material for public display.

Internship
New Mexico State Highway Department
Academic year 2002 to 2003
Worked on a dig at a site slated for new highway construction.

continued

Work-Study Program
Albuquerque Historical Society
Summers 2000, 2001
Worked in the archives, cataloging documents and photographs.

REFERENCES
Both personal and professional references are available upon request.

Choose one of the following types of objective statement:

1. General Objective Statement

- An entry-level educational programming coordinator position

2. Position-Focused Objective

- To obtain the position of conference coordinator at State College

3. Industry-Focused Objective

- To begin a career as a sales representative in the cruise line industry

4. Summary of Qualifications Statement

A degree in anthropology with a concentration in archaeology and three years of progressively increasing responsibilities in the curatorial department of a major museum have prepared me for a career as a curator in an institution that values hands-on involvement and thoroughness.

Support Your Objective. A résumé that contains any one of these types of objective statements should then go on to demonstrate why you are qualified to get the position. Listing academic degrees can be one way to indicate qualifications. Another demonstration would be in the way previous experiences, both volunteer and paid, are described. Without this kind of documentation in the body of the résumé, the objective looks unsupported. Think of the résumé as telling a connected story about you. All the elements should work together to form a coherent picture that ideally should relate to your statement of objective.

Education

This section of your résumé should indicate the exact name of the degree you will receive or have received, spelled out completely with no abbreviations. The degree is generally listed after the objective, followed by the institution name and location, and then the month and year of graduation. This section could also include your academic minor, grade point average (GPA), and appearance on the Dean's List or President's List.

If you have enough space, you might want to include a section listing courses related to the field in which you are seeking work. The best use of a "related courses" section would be to list some course work that is not traditionally associated with the major. Perhaps you took several computer courses outside your degree that will be helpful and related to the job prospects you are entertaining. Several education section examples are shown here:

- Bachelor of Arts in Anthropology
  University of Florida, Gainesville, FL, 2004
  Minor: Language Arts
- Bachelor of Arts in Anthropology
  Boston University, Boston, MA, May 2004
  Concentration: Cultural Anthropology
- Bachelor of Science in Anthropology
  University of Denver, Denver, CO, 2004
  Concentration: Archaeology

An example of a format for a related-courses section follows:

RELATED COURSES	
Photography	Spanish
Computer graphics	Drafting
Architectural design	Research methods

Experience

The experience section of your résumé should be the most substantial part and should take up most of the space on the page. Employers want to see what kind of work history you have. They will look at your range of experiences, longevity in jobs, and specific tasks you are able to complete. This section may also be called "work experience," "related experience," "employment history," or "employment." No matter what you call this section, some important points to remember are the following:

1. **Describe your duties** as they relate to the position you are seeking.
2. **Emphasize major responsibilities** and indicate increases in responsibility. Include all relevant employment experiences: summer, part-time, internships, cooperative education, or self-employment.
3. **Emphasize skills**, especially those that transfer from one situation to another. The fact that you coordinated a student organization, chaired meetings, supervised others, and managed a budget leads one to suspect that you could coordinate other things as well.
4. **Use descriptive job titles** that provide information about what you did. A "Student Intern" should be more specifically stated as, for example, "Magazine Operations Intern." "Volunteer" is also too general; a title such as "Peer Writing Tutor" would be more appropriate.
5. **Create word pictures** by using active verbs to start sentences. Describe *results* you have produced in the work you have done.

A limp description would say something such as the following: "My duties included helping with production, proofreading, and editing. I used a design and page layout program." An action statement would be stated as follows: "Coordinated and assisted in the creative marketing of brochures and seminar promotions, becoming proficient in Quark."

Remember, an accomplishment is simply a result, a final measurable product that people can relate to. A duty is not a result; it is an obligation—every job holder has duties. For an effective résumé, list as many results as you can. To make the most of the limited space you have and to give your description impact, carefully select appropriate and accurate descriptors.

Here are some traits that employers tell us they like to see:

- Teamwork
- Energy and motivation
- Learning and using new skills
- Versatility
- Critical thinking
- Understanding how profits are created
- Organizational acumen

tive stated on your résumé. If you can draw a valid connection between your activities and your objective, include them; if not, leave them out.

Professional affiliations and honors should all be listed; especially important are those related to your job objective. Social clubs and activities need not be a part of your résumé unless you hold a significant office or you are looking for a position related to your membership. Be aware that most prospective employers' principal concerns are related to your employability, not your social life. If you have any, publications can be included as an addendum to your résumé.

How Should I Handle References?

The use of references is considered a part of the interview process, and they should never be listed on a résumé. You would always provide references to a potential employer if requested to, so it is not even necessary to include this section on the résumé if space does not permit. If space is available, it is acceptable to include the following statement:

- REFERENCES:
  Furnished upon request.

The Functional Résumé

The functional résumé departs from a chronological résumé in that it organizes information by specific accomplishments in various settings: previous jobs, volunteer work, associations, and so forth. This type of résumé permits you to stress the substance of your experiences rather than the position titles you have held. You should consider using a functional résumé if you have held a series of similar jobs that relied on the same skills or abilities. There are many good books in which you can find examples of functional résumés, including *How to Write a Winning Resume* or *Resumes Made Easy*.

The Targeted Résumé

The targeted résumé focuses on specific work-related capabilities you can bring to a given position within an organization. Past achievements are listed to highlight your capabilities and the work history section is abbreviated.

Digital Résumés

Today's employers have to manage an enormous number of résumés. One of the most frequent complaints the writers of this series hear from students is the failure of employers to even acknowledge the receipt of a résumé and cover letter. Frequently, the reason for this poor response or nonresponse is the volume of applications received for every job. In an attempt to better manage the considerable labor investment involved in processing large numbers of résumés, many employers are requiring digital submission of résumés. There are two types of digital résumés: those that can be e-mailed or posted to a website, called *electronic résumés*, and those that can be "read" by a computer, commonly called *scannable résumés*. Though the format may be a bit different from the traditional "paper" résumé, the goal of both types of digital résumés is the same—to get you an interview! These résumés must be designed to be "technologically friendly." What that basically means to you is that they should be free of graphics and fancy formatting. (See Exhibit 2.2.)

Electronic Résumés

Sometimes referred to as plain-text résumés, electronic résumés are designed to be e-mailed to an employer or posted to one of many commercial Internet databases such as CareerMosaic.com, America's Job Bank (ajb.dni.us), or Monster.com.

Some technical considerations:

- Electronic résumés must be written in American Standard Code for Information Interchange (ASCII), which is simply a plain-text format. These characters are universally recognized so that every computer can accurately read and understand them. To create an ASCII file of your current résumé, open your document, then save it as a text or ASCII file. This will eliminate all formatting. Edit as needed using your computer's text editor application.
- Use a standard-width typeface. Courier is a good choice because it is the font associated with ASCII in most systems.
- Use a font size of 11 to 14 points. A 12-point font is considered standard.
- Your margin should be left-justified.
- Do not exceed sixty-five characters per line because the word-wrap function doesn't operate in ASCII.

Exhibit 2.2
DIGITAL RÉSUMÉ

CYNTHIA PORTER
333 W. Belmont Ave.
Chicago, IL 60657
Phone: 773/555-8430
E-mail: cyporter@xxx.com

Put your name at the
top on its own line.

Put your phone number
on its own line.

KEYWORD SUMMARY
Museum
Education
B.A., Anthropology

Keywords make your
résumé easier to find in
a database.

WORK EXPERIENCE
Field Museum of Natural History
Chicago, IL
Public Relations Assistant,
Education Department
1999-present

Use a standard-width
typeface.

Use a space between
asterisk and text.

* Develop promotional materials and
write press releases.
* Schedule school tours, coordinating
with the various departments of the museum.
* Research potential programs and
speakers for museum programs.

No line should exceed
sixty-five characters.

Charles Gates Dawes House
Evanston, IL
Assistant to the Director
1997-1999

End each line by
hitting the ENTER
(or RETURN) key.

* Trained and supervised docents.
* Scheduled group tours and led tours
for school groups.
* Managed the House's lecture series.

continued

```
EDUCATION  ◄─────────────────────────────    Capitalize letters to
B.A., Anthropology, 1997                      emphasize headings.
Syracuse University, NY
```

- Do not use boldface, italics, underlining, bullets, or various font sizes. Instead, use asterisks, plus signs, or all capital letters when you want to emphasize something.
- Avoid graphics and shading.
- Use as many "keywords" as you possibly can. These are words or phrases usually relating to skills or experience that either are specifically used in the job announcement or are popular buzzwords in the industry.
- Minimize abbreviations.
- Your name should be the first line of text.
- Conduct a "test run" by e-mailing your résumé to yourself and a friend before you send it to the employer. See how it transmits, and make any changes you need to. Continue to test it until it's exactly how you want it to look.
- Unless an employer specifically requests that you send the résumé in the form of an attachment, don't. Employers can encounter problems opening a document as an attachment, and there are always viruses to consider.
- Don't forget your cover letter. Send it along with your résumé as a single message.

Scannable Résumés

Some companies are relying on technology to narrow the candidate pool for available job openings. Electronic Applicant Tracking uses imaging to scan, sort, and store résumé elements in a database. Then, through OCR (Optical Character Recognition) software, the computer scans the résumés for keywords and phrases. To have the best chance at getting an interview, you want to increase the number of "hits"—matches of your skills, abilities, experience, and education to those the computer is scanning for—your résumé will get. You can see how critical using the right keywords is for this type of résumé.

Technical considerations include:

- Again, do not use boldface (newer systems may read this OK, but many older ones won't), italics, underlining, bullets, shading, graphics, or multiple font sizes. Instead, for emphasis, use asterisks, plus signs, or all capital letters. Minimize abbreviations.

- Use a popular typeface such as Courier, Helvetica, Ariel, or Palatino. Avoid decorative fonts.
- Font size should be between 11 and 14 points.
- Do not compress the spacing between letters.
- Use horizontal and vertical lines sparingly; the computer may misread them as the letters *L* or *I*.
- Left-justify the text.
- Do not use parentheses or brackets around telephone numbers, and be sure your phone number is on its own line of text.
- Your name should be the first line of text and on its own line. If your résumé is longer than one page, be sure to put your name on the top of all pages.
- Use a traditional résumé structure. The chronological format may work best.
- Use nouns that are skill-focused, such as *management*, *writer*, and *programming*. This is different from traditional paper résumés, which use action-oriented verbs.
- Laser printers produce the finest copies. Avoid dot-matrix printers.
- Use standard, light-colored paper with text on one side only. Since the higher the contrast, the better, your best choice is black ink on white paper.
- Always send original copies. If you must fax, set the fax on fine mode, not standard.
- Do not staple or fold your résumé. This can confuse the computer.
- Before you send your scannable résumé, be certain the employer uses this technology. If you can't determine this, you may want to send two versions (scannable and traditional) to be sure your résumé gets considered.

Résumé Production and Other Tips

An ink-jet printer is the preferred option for printing your résumé. Begin by printing just a few copies. You may find a small error or you may simply want to make some changes, and it is less frustrating and less expensive if you print in small batches.

Résumé paper color should be carefully chosen. You should consider the types of employers who will receive your résumé and the types of positions for which you are applying. Use white or ivory paper for traditional or conservative employers or for higher-level positions.

Black ink on sharp, white paper can be harsh on the reader's eyes. Think about an ivory or cream paper that will provide less contrast and be easier to read. Pink, green, and blue tints should generally be avoided.

Many résumé writers buy packages of matching envelopes and cover sheet stationery that, although not absolutely necessary, help convey a professional impression.

If you'll be producing many cover letters at home, be sure you have high-quality printing equipment. Learn standard envelope formats for business, and retain a copy of every cover letter you send out. You can use the copies to take notes of any telephone conversations that may occur.

If attending a job fair, either carry a briefcase or place your résumé in a nicely covered legal-size pad holder.

The Cover Letter

The cover letter provides you with the opportunity to tailor your résumé by telling the prospective employer how you can be a benefit to the organization. It allows you to highlight aspects of your background that are not already discussed in your résumé and that might be especially relevant to the organization you are contacting or to the position you are seeking. Every résumé should have a cover letter enclosed when you send it out. Unlike the résumé, which may be mass-produced, a cover letter is most effective when it is individually prepared and focused on the particular requirements of the organization in question.

A good cover letter should supplement the résumé and motivate the reader to review the résumé. The format shown in Exhibit 2.3 (see page 34) is only a suggestion to help you decide what information to include in a cover letter.

Begin the cover letter with your street address six lines down from the top. Leave three to five lines between the date and the name of the person to whom you are addressing the cover letter. Make sure you leave one blank line between the salutation and the body of the letter and between paragraphs. After typing "Sincerely," leave four blank lines and type your name. This should leave plenty of room for your signature. A sample cover letter is shown in Exhibit 2.4 on page 35.

The following guidelines will help you write good cover letters:

1. Be sure to type your letter neatly; ensure there are no misspellings.
2. Avoid unusual typefaces, such as script.
3. Address the letter to an individual, using the person's name and title. To obtain this information, call the company. If answering a blind newspaper advertisement, address the letter "To Whom It May Concern" or omit the salutation.
4. Be sure your cover letter directly indicates the position you are applying for and tells why you are qualified to fill it.
5. Send the original letter, not a photocopy, with your résumé. Keep a copy for your records.
6. Make your cover letter no more than one page.
7. Include a phone number where you can be reached.
8. Avoid trite language and have someone read the letter over to react to its tone, content, and mechanics.
9. For your own information, record the date you send out each letter and résumé.

Exhibit 2.3
COVER LETTER FORMAT

Your Street Address
Your Town, State, Zip
Phone Number
Fax Number
E-mail

Date

Name
Title
Organization
Address

Dear _____:

First Paragraph. In this paragraph state the reason for the letter, name the specific position or type of work you are applying for, and indicate from which resource (career services office, website, newspaper, contact, employment service) you learned of this opening. The first paragraph can also be used to inquire about future openings.

Second Paragraph. Indicate why you are interested in this position, the company, or its products or services, and what you can do for the employer. If you are a recent graduate, explain how your academic background makes you a qualified candidate. Try not to repeat the same information found in the résumé.

Third Paragraph. Refer the reader to the enclosed résumé for more detailed information.

Fourth Paragraph. In this paragraph say what you will do to follow up on your letter. For example, state that you will call by a certain date to set up an interview or to find out if the company will be recruiting in your area. Finish by indicating your willingness to answer any questions the recipient may have. Be sure you have provided your phone number.

Sincerely,

Type your name
Enclosure

Exhibit 2.4
SAMPLE COVER LETTER

156 Royce Rd., Apt. #3
Allston, MA 02138
(617) 555-2289

May 10, 2004

Heather Peterson
Director of Personnel
Talbert Museum
Boston University
88 The Fenway
Boston, MA 02115

Dear Ms. Peterson:

In June of 2005 I will graduate from Northeastern University with a bachelor of arts degree in anthropology with a minor in museum studies. I read of your opening for an assistant collections manager in the *Globe* on Sunday, May 9, and I am very interested in the possibilities it offers.

The ad indicated that you are looking for creative team players with good communication skills and natural history collection management experience. I believe I possess these qualities. Through my placement at the Hadley Museum of Natural History with Northeastern's cooperative education program, I learned the ins and outs of the workings of a major museum, including the importance of teamwork.

In addition to the anthropology and museum studies courses in my academic program, I felt it important to enroll in related computer courses to learn the use of spreadsheets and databases. This curriculum helped me to become familiar with the wide range of museum collections as well as a variety of computer tracking systems. I believe that these skills, coupled with my enthusiasm for working in a natural history museum environment, will help me to represent Talbert Museum in a professional and creative manner.

As you will see by my enclosed résumé, I worked at the Hadley Museum of Natural History for a total of three years, both in the registrar's office and

continued

under the direction of the curator of nineteenth-century Native American art. These placements provided me with experience in handling and exhibiting objects and paintings and allowed me to see how both offices function cooperatively.

I would like to meet with you to discuss how my education and experience would be consistent with your needs. I will contact your office next week to discuss the possibility of an interview. In the meantime, if you have any questions or require additional information, please contact me at my home at (617) 555-2289.

Sincerely,

Elaine Jacoby

Enclosure

3

Researching Careers and Networking

As an anthropology major, you may have chosen your degree based solely on what you wanted to study, with little thought about what job possibilities awaited you after graduation. Anthropology is a vast field, populated with an almost endless number of job titles, some of which you might not have encountered before. You know that an anthropology major has given you an overview of archaeology and cultural, physical, and linguistic anthropology. However, you still may be confused as to exactly what kinds of organizations will hire you. Are the only jobs slated for Ph.D. holders? Where can an anthropologist fit into a hospital, an automobile manufacturing company, or an environmental learning center?

What Do They Call the Job You Want?

One reason for confusion is perhaps a mistaken assumption that a college education provides job training. In most cases it does not. Of course, applied fields such as engineering, management, or education provide specific skills for the workplace as well as an education. Regardless, your overall college education exposes you to numerous fields of study and teaches you quantitative reasoning, critical thinking, writing, and speaking, all of which can be successfully applied to a number of different job fields. But it still remains up to you to choose a job field and to learn how to articulate the benefits of your education in a way the employer will appreciate.

Collect Job Titles

The world of employment is a complex place, so you need to become a bit of an explorer and adventurer and be willing to try a variety of techniques to develop a list of possible occupations that might use your talents and education. You might find computerized interest inventories, reference books and other sources, and classified ads helpful in this respect. Once you have a list of possibilities that you are interested in and qualified for, you can move on to find out what kinds of organizations have these job titles.

Computerized Interest Inventories. One way to begin collecting job titles is to identify a number of jobs that call for your degree and the particular skills and interests you identified as part of the self-assessment process. There are excellent interactive career-guidance programs on the market to help you produce such selected lists of possible job titles. Most of these are available at colleges and at some larger town and city libraries. Two of the industry leaders are *SIGI Plus* and *DISCOVER*. Both allow you to enter interests, values, educational background, and other information to produce lists of possible occupations and industries. Each of the resources listed here will produce different job title lists. Some job titles will appear again and again, while others will be unique to a particular source. Investigate all of them!

Reference Sources. Books on the market that may be available through your local library or career counseling office also suggest various occupations related to specific majors. The following are only a few of the many good books on the market: *The College Board Guide to 150 Popular College Majors* and *College Majors and Careers: A Resource Guide for Effective Life Planning* by Paul Phifer, and *The College Majors Handbook* by Paul E. Harrington. All of these books list possible job titles within the academic major.

There are dozens of possible job titles for those interested in pursuing a career in anthropology. Some are familiar ones, such as archaeologist or teacher, and others are interestingly different, such as program evaluator or director of research. The Occupational Information Network, or O*Net Online, at http://online.onetcenter.org, is a good resource for researching job titles under general categories. Under "anthropologist," for example, you'll find a list of more than seven associated job titles including sociologist, urban and regional planner, geographer, and

curator. All job titles are cross-referenced to the appropriate
titles in the Department of Labor's *Dictionary of Occupational
Titles*.

Each job title deserves your consideration. Like removing the layers of an
onion, the search for job titles can go on and on! As you spend time doing
this activity, you are actually learning more about the value of your degree.
What's important in your search at this point is not to become critical or
selective but rather to develop as long a list of possibilities as you can. Every
source used will help you add new and potentially exciting jobs to your growing list.

Classified Ads. It has been well publicized that the classified ad section of
the newspaper represents only a small fraction of the current job market. Nevertheless, the weekly classified ads can be a great help to you in your search.
Although they may not be the best place to look for a job, they can teach
you a lot about the job market. Classified ads provide a good education in
job descriptions, duties, responsibilities, and qualifications. In addition, they
provide insight into which industries are actively recruiting and some indication of the area's employment market. This is particularly helpful when
seeking a position in a specific geographic area and/or a specific field. For
your purposes, classified ads are a good source for job titles to add to your
list.

Read the Sunday classified ads in a major market newspaper for several
weeks in a row. Cut and paste all the ads that interest you and seem to call
for something close to your education, skills, experience, and interests.
Remember that classified ads are written for what an organization *hopes* to
find, you don't have to meet absolutely every criterion. However, if certain
requirements are stated as absolute minimums and you cannot meet them,
it's best not to waste your time and that of the employer.

The weekly classified want ads exercise is important because these jobs
are out in the marketplace. They truly exist, and people with your qualifications are being sought to apply. What's more, many of these advertisements
describe the duties and responsibilities of the job advertised and give you a
beginning sense of the challenges and opportunities such a position presents.
Some will indicate salary, and that will be helpful as well. This information
will better define the jobs for you and provide some good material for possible interviews in that field.

Explore Job Descriptions

Once you've arrived at a solid list of possible job titles that interest you and for which you believe you are somewhat qualified, it's a good idea to do some research on each of these jobs. The preeminent source for such job information is the *Dictionary of Occupational Titles*, or *DOT* (wave.net/upg /immigration/dot_index.html). This directory lists every conceivable job and provides excellent up-to-date information on duties and responsibilities, interactions with associates, and day-to-day assignments and tasks. These descriptions provide a thorough job analysis, but they do not consider the possible employers or the environments in which a job may be performed. So, although a position as public relations officer may be well defined in terms of duties and responsibilities, it does not explain the differences in doing public relations work in a college or a hospital or a factory or a bank. You will need to look somewhere else for work settings.

Learn More About Possible Work Settings

After reading some job descriptions, you may choose to edit and revise your list of job titles once again, discarding those you feel are not suitable and keeping those that continue to hold your interest. Or you may wish to keep your list intact and see where these jobs may be located. For example, if you are interested in public relations and you appear to have those skills and the requisite education, you'll want to know what organizations do public relations. How can you find that out? How much income does someone in public relations make a year and what is the employment potential for the field of public relations?

To answer these and many other questions about your list of job titles, we recommend you try one of the following resources: *Careers Encyclopedia*, the professional societies and resources found throughout this book, and the *Occupational Outlook Handbook* (bls.gov/oco). Each of these resources, in a different way, will help to put the job titles you have selected into an employer context. Perhaps the most extensive discussion is found in the *Occupational Outlook Handbook*, which gives a thorough presentation of the nature of the work, the working conditions, employment statistics, training, other qualifications, and advancement possibilities as well as job outlook and earnings. Related occupations are also detailed, and a select bibliography is provided to help you find additional information.

Continuing with our public relations example, your search through these reference materials would teach you that the public relations jobs you find attractive are available in larger hospitals, financial institutions, most corporations (both consumer goods and industrial goods), media organizations, and colleges and universities.

Networking

Networking is the process of deliberately establishing relationships to get career-related information or to alert potential employers that you are available for work. Networking is critically important to today's job seeker for two reasons: it will help you get the information you need, and it can help you find out about *all* of the available jobs.

Get the Information You Need

Networkers will review your résumé and give you feedback on its effectiveness. They will talk about the job you are looking for and give you a candid appraisal of how they see your strengths and weaknesses. If they have a good sense of the industry or the employment sector for that job, you'll get their feelings on future trends in the industry as well. Some networkers will be very forthcoming about salaries, job-hunting techniques, and suggestions for your job search strategy. Many have been known to place calls right from the interview desk to friends and associates who might be interested in you. Each networker will make his or her own contribution, and each will be valuable.

Because organizations must evolve to adapt to current global market needs, the information provided by decision makers within various organizations will be critical to your success as a new job market entrant. For example, you might learn about the concept of virtual organizations from a networker. Virtual organizations coordinate economic activity to deliver value to customers by using resources outside the traditional boundaries of the organization. This concept is being discussed and implemented by chief executive officers of many organizations, including Ford Motor, Dell, and IBM. Networking can help you find out about this and other trends currently affecting the industries under your consideration.

Find Out About All of the Available Jobs

Not every job that is available at this very moment is advertised for potential applicants to see. This is called the *hidden job market*. Only 15 to 20 percent of all jobs are formally advertised, which means that 80 to 85 percent of available jobs do not appear in published channels. Networking will help you become more knowledgeable about all the employment opportunities available during your job search period.

Although someone you might talk to today doesn't know of any openings within his or her organization, tomorrow or next week or next month an opening may occur. If you've taken the time to show an interest in and knowledge of their organization, if you've shown the company representative how you can help achieve organizational goals and that you can fit into the organization, you'll be one of the first candidates considered for the position.

Networking: A Proactive Approach

Networking is a proactive rather than a reactive approach. You, as a job seeker, are expected to initiate a certain level of activity on your own behalf; you cannot afford to simply respond to jobs listed in the newspaper. Being proactive means building a network of contacts that includes informed and interested decision makers who will provide you with up-to-date knowledge of the current job market and increase your chances of finding out about employment opportunities appropriate for your interests, experience, and level of education. An old axiom of networking says, "You are only two phone calls away from the information you need." In other words, by talking to enough people, you will quickly come across someone who can offer you help.

Preparing to Network

In deliberately establishing relationships, maximize your efforts by organizing your approach. Five specific areas in which you can organize your efforts include reviewing your self-assessment, reviewing your research on job sites and organizations, deciding who it is you want to talk to, keeping track of all your efforts, and creating your self-promotion tools.

Review Your Self-Assessment

Your self-assessment is as important a tool in preparing to network as it has been in other aspects of your job search. You have carefully evaluated your personal traits, personal values, economic needs, longer-term goals, skill base, preferred skills, and underdeveloped skills. During the networking process you will be called upon to communicate what you know about yourself and relate it to the information or job you seek. Be sure to review the exercises that you completed in the self-assessment section of this book in preparation for networking. We've explained that you need to assess what skills you have acquired from your major that are of general value to an employer and to be ready to express those in ways employers can appreciate as useful in their own organizations.

Review Research on Job Sites and Organizations

In addition, individuals assisting you will expect that you'll have at least some background information on the occupation or industry of interest to you. Refer to the appropriate sections of this book and other relevant publications to acquire the background information necessary for effective networking. They'll explain how to identify not only the job titles that might be of interest to you but also what kinds of organizations employ people to do that job. You will develop some sense of working conditions and expectations about duties and responsibilities—all of which will be of help in your networking interviews.

Decide Who It Is You Want to Talk To

Networking cannot begin until you decide who it is that you want to talk to and, in general, what type of information you hope to gain from your contacts. Once you know this, it's time to begin developing a list of contacts. Five useful sources for locating contacts are described here.

College Alumni Network. Most colleges and universities have created a formal network of alumni and friends of the institution who are particularly interested in helping currently enrolled students and graduates of their alma mater gain employment-related information.

It is usually a simple process to make use of an alumni network. Visit your college's website and locate the alumni office and/or your career center. Either or both sites will have information about your school's alumni network. You'll be provided with information on shadowing experiences, geographic information, or those alumni offering job referrals. If you don't find what you're looking for, don't hesitate to phone or e-mail your career center and ask what they can do to help you connect with an alum.

Alumni networkers may provide some combination of the following services: day-long shadowing experiences, telephone interviews, in-person interviews, information on relocating to given geographic areas, internship information, suggestions on graduate school study, and job vacancy notices.

Present and Former Supervisors. If you believe you are on good terms with present or former job supervisors, they may be an excellent resource for providing information or directing you to appropriate resources that would have information related to your current interests and needs. Additionally, these supervisors probably belong to professional organizations that they might be willing to utilize to get information for you.

Employers in Your Area. Although you may be interested in working in a geographic location different from the one where you currently reside, don't overlook the value of the knowledge and contacts those around you are able to provide. Use the local telephone directory and newspaper to identify the types of organizations you are thinking of working for or professionals who have the kinds of jobs you are interested in. Recently, a call made to a local hospital's financial administrator for information on working in health-care financial administration yielded more pertinent information on training seminars, regional professional organizations, and potential employment sites than a national organization was willing to provide.

Employers in Geographic Areas Where You Hope to Work. If you are thinking about relocating, identifying prospective employers or informational contacts in the new location will be critical to your success. Here are some tips for online searching. First, use a "metasearch" engine to get the most out of your search. Metasearch engines combine several engines into one powerful tool. We frequently use dogpile.com and metasearch.com for this purpose. Try using the city and state as your keywords in a search. *New Haven, Connecticut* will bring you to the city's website with links to the chamber of commerce, member businesses, and other valuable resources. By using looksmart.com you can locate newspapers in any area, and they, too, can provide valuable insight before you relocate. Of course, both dogpile and metasearch can lead you to yellow and white page directories in areas you are considering.

Professional Associations and Organizations. Professional associations and organizations can provide valuable information in several areas: career paths that you might not have considered, qualifications relating to those career choices, publications that list current job openings, and workshops or seminars that will enhance your professional knowledge and skills. They can also be excellent sources for background information on given industries: their health, current problems, and future challenges.

There are several excellent resources available to help you locate professional associations and organizations that would have information to meet your needs. Two especially useful publications are the *Encyclopedia of Associations* and *National Trade and Professional Associations of the United States.*

Keep Track of All Your Efforts

It can be difficult, almost impossible, to remember all the details related to each contact you make during the networking process, so you will want to develop a record-keeping system that works for you. Formalize this process by using your computer to keep a record of the people and organizations you want to contact. You can simply record the contact's name, address, and telephone number, and what information you hope to gain.

You could record this as a simple Word document and you could still use the "Find" function if you were trying to locate some data and could only recall the firm's name or the contact's name. If you're comfortable with database management and you have some database software on your computer, then you can put information at your fingertips even if you have only the zip code! The point here is not technological sophistication but good record keeping.

Once you have created this initial list, it will be helpful to keep more detailed information as you begin to actually make the contacts. Those details should include complete contact information, the date and content of each contact, names and information for additional networkers, and required follow-up. Don't forget to send a letter thanking your contact for his or her time! Your contact will appreciate your recall of details of your meetings and conversations, and the information will help you to focus your networking efforts.

Create Your Self-Promotion Tools

There are two types of promotional tools that are used in the networking process. The first is a résumé and cover letter, and the second is a one-minute "infomercial," which may be given over the telephone or in person.

Techniques for writing an effective résumé and cover letter are discussed in Chapter 2. Once you have reviewed that material and prepared these important documents, you will have created one of your self-promotion tools.

The one-minute infomercial will demand that you begin tying your interests, abilities, and skills to the people or organizations you want to network with. Think about your goal for making the contact to help you understand what you should say about yourself. You should be able to express yourself easily and convincingly. If, for example, you are contacting an alumnus of your institution to obtain the names of possible employment sites in a distant city, be prepared to discuss why you are interested in moving to that location, the types of jobs you are interested in, and the skills and abilities you possess that will make you a qualified candidate.

To create a meaningful one-minute infomercial, write it out, practice it as if it will be a spoken presentation, rewrite it, and practice it again if necessary until expressing yourself comes easily and is convincing.

Here's a simplified example of an infomercial for use over the telephone:

Hello, Dr. Adams? My name is Jill Connors. I am a recent graduate of State College, and I am just beginning a career in the health-care field. I was a medical anthropology major, and I feel confident that I have many of the skills that I understand are valued in medical anthropology, such as analytical and research skills, computer proficiency, and public speaking ability, as well as experience in community outreach work. I also work well under pressure. I've read that composure can be a real advantage in this industry.

Dr. Adams, I'm calling you because I need more information about the health-care field and particularly how medical anthropologists can contribute. I'm hoping you'll have the time to sit down with me for about half an hour and discuss your perspective on medical anthropology careers. There are so many possible places to get into this field, and I am searching for some advice on which of those settings might be the best bet for my combination of skills and experience.

Would you be willing to do that for me? I would greatly appreciate it. I am available most mornings, if that's convenient for you.

It very well may happen that your employer contact wishes you to communicate by e-mail. The infomercial quoted above could easily be rewritten for an e-mail message. You should "cut and paste" your résumé right into the e-mail text itself.

Other effective self-promotion tools include portfolios for those in the arts, writing professions, or teaching. Portfolios show examples of work, photographs of projects or classroom activities, or certificates and credentials that are job related. There may not be an opportunity to use the portfolio during an interview, and it is not something that should be left with the organization. It is designed to be explained and displayed by the creator. However, during some networking meetings, there may be an opportunity to illustrate a point or strengthen a qualification by exhibiting the portfolio.

Beginning the Networking Process

Set the Tone for Your Communications
It can be useful to establish "tone words" for any communications you embark upon. Before making your first telephone call or writing your first letter, decide what you want the person to think of you. If you are networking to try to obtain a job, your tone words might include descriptors such as *genuine*, *informed*, and *self-knowledgeable*. When you're trying to acquire information, your tone words may have a slightly different focus, such as *courteous*, *organized*, *focused*, and *well-spoken*. Use the tone words you establish for your contacts to guide you through the networking process.

Honestly Express Your Intentions
When contacting individuals, it is important to be honest about your reasons for making the contact. Establish your purpose in your own mind and be able and ready to articulate it concisely. Determine an initial agenda, whether it be informational questioning or self-promotion, present it to your contact, and be ready to respond immediately. If you don't adequately prepare before initiating your overture, you may find yourself at a disadvantage if you're asked to immediately begin your informational interview or self-promotion during the first phone conversation or visit.

Start Networking Within Your Circle of Confidence
Once you have organized your approach—by utilizing specific researching methods, creating a system for keeping track of the people you will contact, and developing effective self-promotion tools—you are ready to begin networking. The best way to begin networking is by talking with a group of people you trust and feel comfortable with. This group is usually made up of your family, friends, and career counselors. No matter who is in this inner circle, they will have a special interest in seeing you succeed in your job

search. In addition, because they will be easy to talk to, you should try taking some risks in terms of practicing your information-seeking approach. Gain confidence in talking about the strengths you bring to an organization and the underdeveloped skills you feel hinder your candidacy. Be sure to review the section on self-assessment for tips on approaching each of these areas. Ask for critical but constructive feedback from the people in your circle of confidence on the letters you write and the one-minute infomercial you have developed. Evaluate whether you want to make the changes they suggest, then practice the changes on others within this circle.

Stretch the Boundaries of Your Networking Circle of Confidence

Once you have refined the promotional tools you will use to accomplish your networking goals, you will want to make additional contacts. Because you will not know most of these people, it will be a less comfortable activity to undertake. The practice that you gained with your inner circle of trusted friends should have prepared you to now move outside of that comfort zone.

It is said that any information a person needs is only two phone calls away, but the information cannot be gained until you (1) make a reasonable guess about who might have the information you need and (2) pick up the telephone to make the call. Using your network list that includes alumni, instructors, supervisors, employers, and associations, you can begin preparing your list of questions that will allow you to get the information you need.

Prepare the Questions You Want to Ask

Networkers can provide you with the insider's perspective on any given field and you can ask them questions that you might not want to ask in an interview. For example, you can ask them to describe the more repetitious or mundane parts of the job or ask them for a realistic idea of salary expectations. Be sure to prepare your questions ahead of time so that you are organized and efficient.

Be Prepared to Answer Some Questions

To communicate effectively, you must anticipate questions that will be asked of you by the networkers you contact. Revisit the self-assessment process you undertook and the research you've done so that you can effortlessly respond to questions about your short- and long-term goals and the kinds of jobs you are most interested in pursuing.

General Networking Tips

Make Every Contact Count. Setting the tone for each interaction is critical. Approaches that will help you communicate in an effective way include politeness, being appreciative of time provided to you, and being prepared and thorough. Remember, *everyone* within an organization has a circle of influence, so be prepared to interact effectively with each person you encounter in the networking process, including secretarial and support staff. Many information or job seekers have thwarted their own efforts by being rude to some individuals they encountered as they networked because they made the incorrect assumption that certain persons were unimportant.

Sometimes your contacts may be surprised at their ability to help you. After meeting and talking with you, they might think they have not offered much in the way of help. A day or two later, however, they may make a contact that would be useful to you and refer you to that person.

With Each Contact, Widen Your Circle of Networkers. Always leave an informational interview with the names of at least two more people who can help you get the information or job that you are seeking. Don't be shy about asking for additional contacts; networking is all about increasing the number of people you can interact with to achieve your goals.

Make Your Own Decisions. As you talk with different people and get answers to the questions you pose, you may hear conflicting information or get conflicting suggestions. Your job is to listen to these "experts" and decide what information and which suggestions will help you achieve *your* goals. Only implement those suggestions that you believe will work for you.

Shutting Down Your Network

As you achieve the goals that motivated your networking activity—getting the information you need or the job you want—the time will come to inactivate all or parts of your network. As you do, be sure to tell your primary supporters about your change in status. Call or write to each one of them and give them as many details about your new status as you feel is necessary to maintain a positive relationship.

Because a network takes on a life of its own, activity undertaken on your behalf will continue even after you cease your efforts. As you get calls or are contacted in some fashion, be sure to inform these networkers about your change in status, and thank them for assistance they have provided.

Information on the latest employment trends indicates that workers will change jobs or careers several times in their lifetime. Networking, then, will be a critical aspect in the span of your professional life. If you carefully and thoughtfully conduct your networking activities during your job search, you will have a solid foundation of experience when you need to network the next time around.

Where Are These Jobs, Anyway?

Having a list of job titles that you've designed around your own career interests and skills is an excellent beginning. It means you've really thought about who you are and what you are presenting to the employment market. It has caused you to think seriously about the most appealing environments to work in, and you have identified some employer types that represent these environments.

The research and the thinking that you've done thus far will be used again and again. They will be helpful in writing your résumé and cover letters, in talking about yourself on the telephone to prospective employers, and in answering interview questions.

Now is a good time to begin to narrow the field of job titles and employment sites down to some specific employers to initiate the employment contact.

Find Out Which Employers Hire People Like You

This section will provide tips, techniques, and specific resources for developing an actual list of specific employers that can be used to make contacts. It is only an outline that you must be prepared to tailor to your own particular needs and according to what you bring to the job search. Once again, it is important to communicate with others along the way exactly what you're looking for and what your goals are for the research you're doing. Librarians, employers, career counselors, friends, friends of friends, business contacts, and bookstore staff will all have helpful information on geographically specific and new resources to aid you in locating employers who'll hire you.

Identify Information Resources

Your interview wardrobe and your new résumé might have put a dent in your wallet, but the resources you'll need to pursue your job search are available for free. The categories of information detailed here are not hard to find and are yours for the browsing.

Numerous resources described in this section will help you identify actual employers. Use all of them or any others that you identify as available in your geographic area. As you become experienced in this process, you'll quickly figure out which information sources are helpful and which are not. If you live in a rural area, a well-planned day trip to a major city that includes a college career office, a large college or city library, state and federal employment centers, a chamber of commerce office, and a well-stocked bookstore can produce valuable results.

There are many excellent resources available to help you identify actual job sites. They are categorized into employer directories (usually indexed by product lines and geographic location), geographically based directories (designed to highlight particular cities, regions, or states), career-specific directories (e.g., *Sports MarketPlace*, which lists tens of thousands of firms involved with sports), periodicals and newspapers, targeted job posting publications, and videos. This is by no means meant to be a complete treatment of resources but rather a starting point for identifying useful resources.

Working from the more general references to highly specific resources, we provide a basic list to help you begin your search. Many of these you'll find easily available. In some cases reference librarians and others will suggest even better materials for your particular situation. Start to create your own customized bibliography of job search references.

Geographically Based Directories. The Job Bank series published by Adams Media (adamsmedia.com) contains detailed entries on each area's major employers, including business activity, address, phone number, and hiring contact name. Many listings specify educational backgrounds being sought in potential employees. Each volume contains a solid discussion of each city's or state's major employment sectors. Organizations are also indexed by industry. Job Bank volumes are available for the following places: Atlanta, Boston, Chicago, Dallas–Ft. Worth, Denver, Detroit, Florida, Houston, Los Angeles, Minneapolis, New York, Ohio, Philadelphia, San Francisco, Seattle, St. Louis, Washington, D.C., and other cities throughout the Northwest.

National Job Bank (careercity.com) lists employers in every state, along with contact names and commonly hired job categories. Included are many small companies often overlooked by other directories. Companies are also indexed by industry. This publication provides information on educational backgrounds sought and lists company benefits.

Periodicals and Newspapers. Several sources are available to help you locate which journals or magazines carry job advertisements in your field. Other resources help you identify opportunities in other parts of the country.

- *Where the Jobs Are: A Comprehensive Directory of 1200 Journals Listing Career Opportunities*
- *The Federal Jobs Digest* (jobsfed.com) and *Federal Career Opportunities*
- *World Chamber of Commerce Directory* (chamberofcommerce.com)

This list is certainly not exhaustive; use it to begin your job search work.

Targeted Job Posting Publications. Although the resources that follow are national in scope, they are either targeted to one medium of contact (telephone), focused on specific types of jobs, or less comprehensive than the sources previously listed.

- Careers.org (careers.org/index.html)
- *The Job Hunter* (jobhunter.com)
- *Current Jobs for Graduates* (graduatejobs.com)
- *Environmental Career Opportunities* (ecojobs.com)
- *Y National Vacancy List* (ymca.net/employment/ymca_recruiting/jobright.htm)
- *ArtSEARCH*
- *Community Jobs*
- *National Association of Colleges and Employers: Job Choices series*
- *National Association of Colleges and Employers* (jobweb.com)

Videos. You may be one of the many job seekers who likes to get information via a medium other than paper. Many career libraries, public libraries, and career centers in libraries carry an assortment of videos that will help you learn new techniques and get information helpful in the job search.

Locate Information Resources

Throughout these introductory chapters, we have continually referred you to various websites for information on everything from job listings to career information. Using the Web gives you a mobility at your computer that you don't enjoy if you rely solely on books or newspapers or printed journals. Moreover, material on the Web, if the site is maintained, can be the most up-to-date information available.

You'll eventually identify the information resources that work best for you, but make certain you've covered the full range of resources before you begin to rely on a smaller list. Here's a short list of informational sites that many job seekers find helpful:

- Public and college libraries
- College career centers
- Bookstores
- The Internet
- Local and state government personnel offices
- Career/job fairs

Each one of these sites offers a collection of resources that will help you get the information you need.

As you meet and talk with service professionals at all these sites, be sure to let them know what you're doing. Inform them of your job search, what you've already accomplished, and what you're looking for. The more people who know you're job seeking, the greater the possibility that someone will have information or know someone who can help you along your way.

4

Interviewing and Job Offer Considerations

Certainly, there can be no one part of the job search process more fraught with anxiety and worry than the interview. Yet seasoned job seekers welcome the interview and will often say, "Just get me an interview and I'm on my way!" They understand that the interview is crucial to the hiring process and equally crucial for them, as job candidates, to have the opportunity of a personal dialogue to add to what the employer may already have learned from the résumé, cover letter, and telephone conversations.

Believe it or not, the interview is to be welcomed, and even enjoyed! It is a perfect opportunity for you, the candidate, to sit down with an employer and express yourself and display who you are and what you want. Of course, it takes thought and planning and a little strategy; after all, it *is* a job interview! But it can be a positive, if not pleasant, experience and one you can look back on and feel confident about your performance and effort.

For many new job seekers, a job, any job, seems a wonderful thing. But seasoned interview veterans know that the job interview is an important step for both sides—the employer and the candidate—to see what each has to offer and whether there is going to be a "fit" of personalities, work styles, and attitudes. And it is this concept of balance in the interview, that both sides have important parts to play, that holds the key to success in mastering this aspect of the job search strategy.

Try to think of the interview as a conversation between two interested and equal partners. You both have important, even vital, information to deliver and to learn. Of course, there's no denying the employer has some leverage, especially in the initial interview for recruitment or any interview scheduled by the candidate and not the recruiter. That should not prevent the interviewee from seeking to play an equal part in what should be a fair exchange of information. Too often the untutored candidate allows the interview to become one-sided. The employer asks all the questions and the candidate simply responds. The ideal would be for two mutually interested parties to sit down and discuss possibilities for each. This is a conversation of significance, and it requires preparation, thought about the tone of the interview, and planning of the nature and details of the information to be exchanged.

Preparing for the Interview

The length of most initial interviews is about thirty minutes. Given the brevity, the information that is exchanged ought to be important. The candidate should be delivering material that the employer cannot discover on the résumé, and in turn, the candidate should be learning things about the employer that he or she could not otherwise find out. After all, if you have only thirty minutes, why waste time on information that is already published? The information exchanged is more than just factual, and both sides will learn much from what they see of each other, as well. How the candidate looks, speaks, and acts are important to the employer. The employer's attention to the interview and awareness of the candidate's résumé, the setting, and the quality of information presented are important to the candidate.

Just as the employer has every right to be disappointed when a prospect is late for the interview, looks unkempt, and seems ill-prepared to answer fairly standard questions, the candidate may be disappointed with an interviewer who isn't ready for the meeting, hasn't learned the basic résumé facts, and is constantly interrupted by telephone calls. In either situation there's good reason to feel let down.

There are many elements to a successful interview, and some of them are not easy to describe or prepare for. Sometimes there is just a chemistry between interviewer and interviewee that brings out the best in both, and a good exchange takes place. But there is much the candidate can do to pave the way for success in terms of his or her résumé, personal appearance, goals, and interview strategy—each of which we will discuss. However, none of this preparation is as important as the time and thought the candidate gives to personal self-assessment.

Self-Assessment
Neither a stunning résumé nor an expensive, well-tailored suit can compensate for candidates who do not know what they want, where they are going,

or why they are interviewing with a particular employer. Self-assessment, the process by which we begin to know and acknowledge our own particular blend of education, experiences, needs, and goals, is not something that can be sorted out the weekend before a major interview. Of all the elements of interview preparation, this one requires the longest lead time and cannot be faked.

Because the time allotted for most interviews is brief, it is all the more important for job candidates to understand and express succinctly why they are there and what they have to offer. This is not a time for undue modesty (or for braggadocio either); it is a time for a compelling, reasoned statement of why you feel that you and this employer might make a good match. It means you have to have thought about your skills, interests, and attributes; related those to your life experiences and your own history of challenges and opportunities; and determined what that indicates about your strengths, preferences, values, and areas needing further development.

If you need some assistance with self-assessment issues, refer to Chapter 1. Included are suggested exercises that can be done as needed, such as making up an experiential diary and extracting obvious strengths and weaknesses from past experiences. These simple assignments will help you look at past activities as collections of tasks with accompanying skills and responsibilities. Don't overlook your high school or college career office. Many offer personal counseling on self-assessment issues and may provide testing instruments such as the *Myers-Briggs Type Indicator (MBTI)*, the *Harrington-O'Shea Career Decision-Making System (CDM)*, the *Strong Interest Inventory (SII)*, or any other of a wide selection of assessment tools that can help you clarify some of these issues prior to the interview stage of your job search.

The Résumé

Résumé preparation has been discussed in detail, and some basic examples were provided. In this section we want to concentrate on how best to use your résumé in the interview. In most cases the employer will have seen the résumé prior to the interview, and, in fact, it may well have been the quality of that résumé that secured the interview opportunity.

An interview is a conversation, however, and not an exercise in reading. So, if the employer hasn't seen your résumé and you have brought it along to the interview, wait until asked or until the end of the interview to offer it. Otherwise, you may find yourself staring at the back of your résumé and simply answering "yes" and "no" to a series of questions drawn from that document.

Sometimes an interviewer is not prepared and does not know or recall the contents of the résumé and may use the résumé to a greater or lesser degree as a "prompt" during the interview. It is for you to judge what that may indicate about the individual performing the interview or the employer. If your interviewer seems surprised by the scheduled meeting, relies on the résumé to an inordinate degree, and seems otherwise unfamiliar with your background, this lack of preparation for the hiring process could well be a symptom of general management disorganization or may simply be the result of poor planning on the part of one individual. It is your responsibility as a potential employee to be aware of these signals and make your decisions accordingly.

If you find that the interviewer is reading from your résumé rather than discussing the job with you, you can guide the interviewer back to the job dialogue by saying, "Mr. Davis, I would like to elaborate on some recent research experience that isn't detailed on my résumé." This strategy may give you an opportunity to convey more information about your strengths and experiences and will reengage the direction of your interview.

By all means, bring at least one copy of your résumé to the interview. Occasionally, at the close of an interview, an interviewer will express an interest in circulating a résumé to several departments, and you could then offer the copy you brought. Sometimes, an interview appointment provides an opportunity to meet others in the organization who may express an interest in you and your background, and it may be helpful to follow up with a copy of your résumé. Our best advice, however, is to keep it out of sight until needed or requested.

Employer Information

Whether your interview is for graduate school admission, an overseas corporate position, or a position with a local company, it is important to know something about the employer or the organization. Keeping in mind that the interview is relatively brief and that you will hopefully have other interviews with other organizations, it is important to keep your research in proportion. If secondary interviews are called for, you will have additional time to do further research. For the first interview, it is helpful to know the organization's mission, goals, size, scope of operations, and so forth. Your research may uncover recent areas of challenge or particular successes that may help to fuel the interview. Use the "What Do They Call the Job You Want?" section of Chapter 3, your library, and your career or guidance office to help you locate this information in the most efficient way possible. Don't be shy in asking advice of these counseling and guidance professionals on how best to spend your preparation time. With some practice, you'll soon learn how much information is enough and which kinds of information are most useful to you.

Interview Content

We've already discussed how it can help to think of the interview as an important conversation—one that, as with any conversation, you want to find pleasant and interesting and to leave you with a good feeling. But because this conversation is especially important, the information that's exchanged is critical to its success. What do you want them to know about you? What do you need to know about them? What interview technique do you need to particularly pay attention to? How do you want to manage the close of the interview? What steps will follow in the hiring process?

Except for the professional interviewer, most of us find interviewing stressful and anxiety-provoking. Developing a strategy before you begin interviewing will help you relieve some stress and anxiety. One particular strategy that has worked for many and may work for you is interviewing by objective. Before you interview, write down three to five goals you would like to achieve for that interview. They may be technique goals: smile a little more, have a firmer handshake, be sure to ask about the next stage in the interview process before leaving. They may be content-oriented goals: find out about the company's current challenges and opportunities; be sure to speak of your recent research, writing experiences, or foreign travel. Whatever your goals, jot down a few of them as goals for each interview.

Most people find that in trying to achieve these few goals, their interviewing technique becomes more organized and focused. After the interview, the most common question friends and family ask is "How did it go?" With this technique, you have an indication of whether you met *your* goals for the meeting, not just some vague idea of how it went. Chances are, if you accomplished what you wanted to, it improved the quality of the entire interview. As you continue to interview, you will want to revise your goals to continue improving your interview skills.

Now, add to the concept of the significant conversation the idea of a beginning, a middle, and a closing and you will have two thoughts that will give your interview a distinctive character. Be sure to make your introduction warm and cordial. Say your full name (and if it's a difficult-to-pronounce name, help the interviewer to pronounce it) and make certain you know your interviewer's name and how to pronounce it. Most interviews begin with some "soft talk" about the weather, chat about the candidate's trip to the interview site, or national events. This is done as a courtesy to relax both you and the interviewer, to get you talking, and to generally try to defuse the atmosphere of excessive tension. Try to be yourself, engage in the conversation, and don't try to second-guess the interviewer. This is simply what it appears to be—casual conversation.

Once you and the interviewer move on to exchange more serious information in the middle part of the interview, the two most important concerns become your ability to handle challenging questions and your success at asking meaningful ones. Interviewer questions will probably fall into one of three categories: personal assessment and career direction, academic assessment, and knowledge of the employer. Here are a few examples of questions in each category:

Personal Assessment and Career Direction
1. What motivates you to put forth your best effort?
2. What do you consider to be your greatest strengths and weaknesses?
3. What qualifications do you have that make you think you will be successful in this career?

Academic Assessment
1. What led you to choose your major?
2. What subjects did you like best and least? Why?
3. How has your college experience prepared you for this career?

Knowledge of the Employer
1. What do you think it takes to be successful in an organization like ours?
2. In what ways do you think you can make a contribution to our organization?
3. Why did you choose to seek a position with this organization?

The interviewer wants a response to each question but is also gauging your enthusiasm, preparedness, and willingness to communicate. In each response you should provide some information about yourself that can be related to the employer's needs. A common mistake is to give too much information. Answer each question completely, but be careful not to run on too long with extensive details or examples.

Questions About Underdeveloped Skills

Most employers interview people who have met some minimum criteria of education and experience. They interview candidates to see who they are, to learn what kind of personality they exhibit, and to get some sense of how this person might fit into the existing organization. It may be that you are asked about skills the employer hopes to find and that you have not documented. Maybe it's grant-writing experience, knowledge of the European political system, or a knowledge of the film world.

To questions about skills and experiences you don't have, answer honestly and forthrightly and try to offer some additional information about skills you do have. For example, perhaps the employer is disappointed you have no grant-writing experience. An honest answer may be as follows:

> *No, unfortunately, I was never in a position to acquire those skills. I do understand something of the complexities of the grant-writing process and feel confident that my attention to detail, careful reading skills, and strong writing would make grants a wonderful challenge in a new job. I think I could get up on the learning curve quickly.*

The employer hears an honest admission of lack of experience but is reassured by some specific skill details that do relate to grant writing and a confident manner that suggests enthusiasm and interest in a challenge.

For many students, questions about their possible contribution to an employer's organization can prove challenging. Because your education has probably not included specific training for a job, you need to review your academic record and select capabilities you have developed in your major that an employer can appreciate. For example, perhaps you read well and can analyze and condense what you've read into smaller, more focused pieces. That could be valuable. Or maybe you did some serious research and you know you have valuable investigative skills. Your public speaking might be highly developed and you might use visual aids appropriately and effectively. Or maybe your skill at correspondence, memos, and messages is effective. Whatever it is, you must take it out of the academic context and put it into a new, employer-friendly context so your interviewer can best judge how you could help the organization.

Exhibiting knowledge of the organization will, without a doubt, show the interviewer that you are interested enough in the available position to have done some legwork in preparation for the interview. Remember, it is not necessary to know every detail of the organization's history but rather to have a general knowledge about why it is in business and how the industry is faring.

Sometime during the interview, generally after the midway point, you'll be asked if you have any questions for the interviewer. Your questions will tell the employer much about your attitude and your desire to understand the organization's expectations so you can compare them to your own strengths. The following are just a few questions you might want to ask:

1. What is the communication style of the organization? (meetings, memos, and so forth)
2. What would a typical day in this position be like for me?
3. What have been some of the interesting challenges and opportunities your organization has recently faced?

Most interviews draw to a natural closing point, so be careful not to prolong the discussion. At a signal from the interviewer, wind up your presentation, express your appreciation for the opportunity, and be sure to ask what the next stage in the process will be. When can you expect to hear from them? Will they be conducting second-tier interviews? If you are interested and haven't heard, would they mind a phone call? Be sure to collect a business card with the name and phone number of your interviewer. On your way out, you might have an opportunity to pick up organizational literature you haven't seen before.

With the right preparation—a thorough self-assessment, professional clothing, and employer information—you'll be able to set and achieve the goals you have established for the interview process.

Interview Follow-Up

Quite often there is a considerable time lag between interviewing for a position and being hired or, in the case of the networker, between your phone call or letter to a possible contact and the opportunity of a meeting. This can be frustrating. "Why aren't they contacting me?" "I thought I'd get another interview, but no one has telephoned." "Am I out of the running?" You don't know what is happening.

Consider the Differing Perspectives

Of course, there is another perspective—that of the networker or hiring organization. Organizations are complex, with multiple tasks that need to be accomplished each day. Hiring is a discrete activity that does not occur as frequently as other job assignments. The hiring process might have to take second place to other, more immediate organizational needs. Although it may be very important to you, and it is certainly ultimately significant to the employer, other issues such as fiscal management, planning and product development, employer vacation periods, or financial constraints may prevent an organization or individual within that organization from acting on your employment or your request for information as quickly as you or they would prefer.

Use Your Communication Skills

Good communication is essential here to resolve any anxieties, and the responsibility is on you, the job or information seeker. Too many job seekers and networkers offer as an excuse that they don't want to "bother" the organization by writing letters or calling. Let us assure you here and now, once and for all, that if you are troubling an organization by over-communicating, someone will indicate that situation to you quite clearly. If not, you can only assume you are a worthwhile prospect and the employer appreciates being reminded of your availability and interest. Let's look at follow-up practices in the job interview process and the networking situation separately.

Following Up on the Employment Interview

A brief thank-you note following an interview is an excellent and polite way to begin a series of follow-up communications with a potential employer with whom you have interviewed and want to remain in touch. It should be just that—a thank-you for a good meeting. If you failed to mention some fact or experience during your interview that you think might add to your candidacy, you may use this note to do that. However, this should be essentially a note whose overall tone is appreciative and, if appropriate, indicative of a continuing interest in pursuing any opportunity that may exist with that organization. It is one of the few pieces of business correspondence that may be handwritten, but always use plain, good-quality, standard-size paper.

If, however, at this point you are no longer interested in the employer, the thank-you note is an appropriate time to indicate that. You are under no obligation to identify any reason for not continuing to pursue employment with that organization, but if you are so inclined to indicate your professional reasons (pursuing other employers more akin to your interests, looking for greater income production than this employer can provide, a different geographic location), you certainly may. It should not be written with an eye to negotiation, for it will not be interpreted as such.

As part of your interview closing, you should have taken the initiative to establish lines of communication for continuing information about your candidacy. If you asked permission to telephone, wait a week following your thank-you note, then telephone your contact simply to inquire how things are progressing on your employment status. The feedback you receive here should be taken at face value. If your interviewer simply has no information, he or she will tell you so and indicate whether you should call again and when. Don't be discouraged if this should continue over some period of time.

If during this time something occurs that you think improves or changes your candidacy (some new qualification or experience you may have had), including any offers from other organizations, by all means telephone or write to inform the employer about this. In the case of an offer from a competing but less desirable or equally desirable organization, telephone your contact, explain what has happened, express your real interest in the organization, and inquire whether some determination on your employment might be made before you must respond to this other offer. An organization that is truly interested in you may be moved to make a decision about your candidacy. Equally possible is the scenario in which they are not yet ready to make a decision and so advise you to take the offer that has been presented. Again, you have no ethical alternative but to deal with the information presented in a straightforward manner.

When accepting other employment, be sure to contact any employers still actively considering you and inform them of your new job. Thank them graciously for their consideration. There are many other job seekers out there just like you who will benefit from having their candidacy improved when others bow out of the race. Who knows, you might at some future time have occasion to interact professionally with one of the organizations with which you sought employment. How embarrassing it would be to have someone remember you as the candidate who failed to notify them that you were taking a job elsewhere!

In all of your follow-up communications, keep good notes of whom you spoke with, when you called, and any instructions that were given about return communications. This will prevent any misunderstandings and provide you with good records of what has transpired.

Job Offer Considerations

For many recent college graduates, the thrill of their first job and, for some, the most substantial regular income they have ever earned seems an excess of good fortune coming at once. To question that first income or to be critical in any way of the conditions of employment at the time of the initial offer seems like looking a gift horse in the mouth. It doesn't seem to occur to many new hires even to attempt to negotiate any aspect of their first job. And, as many employers who deal with entry-level jobs for recent college graduates will readily confirm, the reality is that there simply isn't much movement in salary available to these new college recruits. The entry-level hire generally does not have an employment track record on a professional level to provide any leverage for negotiation. Real negotiations on salary, benefits, retirement provisions, and so forth come to those with significant employment records at higher income levels.

Of course, the job offer is more than just money. It can be composed of geographic assignment, duties and responsibilities, training, benefits, health and medical insurance, educational assistance, car allowance or company vehicle, and a host of other items. All of this is generally detailed in the formal letter that presents the final job offer. In most cases this is a follow-up to a personal phone call from the employer representative who has been principally responsible for your hiring process.

That initial telephone offer is certainly binding as a verbal agreement, but most firms follow up with a detailed letter outlining the most significant parts of your employment contract. You may, of course, choose to respond immediately at the time of the telephone offer (which would be considered a binding oral contract), but you will also be required to formally answer the letter of offer with a letter of acceptance, restating the salient elements of the employer's description of your position, salary, and benefits. This ensures that both parties are clear on the terms and conditions of employment and remuneration and any other outstanding aspects of the job offer.

Is This the Job You Want?

Most new employees will respond affirmatively in writing, glad to be in the position to accept employment. If you've worked hard to get the offer and the job market is tight, other offers may not be in sight, so you will say, "Yes, I accept!" What is important here is that the job offer you accept be one that does fit your particular needs, values, and interests as you've outlined them in your self-assessment process. Moreover, it should be a job that will not only use your skills and education but also challenge you to develop new skills and talents.

Jobs are sometimes accepted too hastily, for the wrong reasons, and without proper scrutiny by the applicant. For example, an individual might readily accept a sales job only to find the continual rejection by potential clients unendurable. An office worker might realize within weeks the constraints of a desk job and yearn for more activity. Employment is an important part of our lives. It is, for most of our adult lives, our most continuous productive activity. We want to make good choices based on the right criteria.

If you have a low tolerance for risk, a job based on commission will certainly be very anxiety-provoking. If being near your family is important, issues of relocation could present a decision crisis for you. If you're an adventurous person, a job with frequent travel would provide needed excitement and be very desirable. The importance of income, the need to continue your education, your personal health situation—all of these have an impact on whether the job you are considering will ultimately meet your needs. Unless you've spent some time understanding and thinking about these issues, it will be difficult to evaluate offers you do receive.

More important, if you make a decision that you cannot tolerate and feel you must leave that job, you will then have both unemployment and self-esteem issues to contend with. These will combine to make the next job search tough going, indeed. So make your acceptance a carefully considered decision.

Negotiate Your Offer

It may be that there is some aspect of your job offer that is not particularly attractive to you. Perhaps there is no relocation allotment to help you move your possessions, and this presents some financial hardship for you. It may be that the health insurance is less than you had hoped. Your initial assignment may be different from what you expected, either in its location or in the duties and responsibilities that comprise it. Or it may simply be that the salary is less than you anticipated. Other considerations may be your official starting date of employment, vacation time, evening hours, dates of training programs or schools, and other concerns.

If you are considering not accepting the job because of some item or items in the job offer "package" that do not meet your needs, you should know that most employers emphatically wish that you would bring that issue to their attention. It may be that the employer can alter it to make the offer more agreeable for you. In some cases it cannot be changed. In any event the employer would generally like to have the opportunity to try to remedy a difficulty rather than risk losing a good potential employee over an issue that might have been resolved. After all, they have spent time and funds in securing your services, and they certainly deserve an opportunity to resolve any possible differences.

Honesty is the best approach in discussing any objections or uneasiness you might have over the employer's offer. Having received your formal offer in writing, contact your employer representative and indicate your particular dissatisfaction in a straightforward manner. For example, you might explain that while you are very interested in being employed by this organization, the salary (or any other benefit) is less than you have determined you require. State the terms you need, and listen to the response. You may be asked to put this in writing, or you may be asked to hold off until the firm can decide on a response. If you are dealing with a senior representative of the organization, one who has been involved in hiring for some time, you may get an immediate response or a solid indication of possible outcomes.

Perhaps the issue is one of relocation. Your initial assignment is in the Midwest, and because you had indicated a strong West Coast preference, you are surprised at the actual assignment. You might simply indicate that while you understand the need for the company to assign you based on its needs, you are disappointed and had hoped to be placed on the West Coast. You could inquire if that were still possible and, if not, would it be reasonable to expect a West Coast relocation in the future.

If your request is presented in a reasonable way, most employers will not see this as jeopardizing your offer. If they can agree to your proposal, they will. If not, they will simply tell you so, and you may choose to continue your candidacy with them or remove yourself from consideration. The choice will be up to you.

Some firms will adjust benefits within their parameters to meet the candidate's need if at all possible. If a candidate requires a relocation cost allowance, he or she may be asked to forgo tuition benefits for the first year to accomplish this adjustment. An increase in life insurance may be adjusted by some other benefit trade-off; perhaps a family dental plan is not needed. In these decisions you are called upon, sometimes under time pressure, to know how you value these issues and how important each is to you.

Many employers find they are more comfortable negotiating for candidates who have unique qualifications or who bring especially needed expertise to the organization. Employers hiring large numbers of entry-level college graduates may be far more reluctant to accommodate any changes in offer conditions. They are well supplied with candidates with similar education and experience so that if rejected by one candidate, they can draw new candidates from an ample labor pool.

Compare Offers

The condition of the economy, the job seeker's academic major and particular geographic job market, and individual needs and demands for certain employment conditions may not provide more than one job offer at a time. Some job seekers may feel that no reasonable offer should go unaccepted for the simple fear there won't be another.

In a tough job market, or if the job you seek is not widely available, or when your job search goes on too long and becomes difficult to sustain financially and emotionally, it may be necessary to accept an inferior offer. The alternative is continued unemployment. Even here, when you feel you don't have a choice, you can at least understand that in accepting this particular offer, there may be limitations and conditions you don't appreciate. At the time of acceptance, there were no other alternatives, but you can begin to use that position to gain the experience and talent to move toward a more attractive position.

Sometimes, however, more than one offer is received, and the candidate has the luxury of choice. If the job seeker knows what he or she wants and has done the necessary self-assessment honestly and thoroughly, it may be clear that one of the offers conforms more closely to those expressed wants and needs.

However, if, as so often happens, the offers are similar in terms of conditions and salary, the question then becomes which organization might provide the necessary climate, opportunities, and advantages for your professional development and growth. This is the time when solid employer research and astute questioning during the interviews really pays off. How much did you learn about the employer through your own research and skillful questioning? When the interviewer asked during the interview "Do you have any questions?" did you ask the kinds of questions that would help resolve a choice between one organization and another? Just as an employer must decide among numerous applicants, so must the applicant learn to assess the potential employer. Both are partners in the job search.

Reneging on an Offer

An especially disturbing occurrence for employers and career counseling professionals is when a job seeker formally (either orally or by written contract) accepts employment with one organization and later reneges on the agreement and goes with another employer.

There are all kinds of rationalizations offered for this unethical behavior. None of them satisfies. The sad irony is that what the job seeker is willing to do to the employer—make a promise and then break it—he or she would be outraged to have done to him- or herself: have the job offer pulled. It is a very bad way to begin a career. It suggests the individual has not taken the time to do the necessary self-assessment and self-awareness exercises to think and judge critically. The new offer taken may, in fact, be no better or worse than the one refused. You should be aware that there have been incidents of legal action following job candidates' reneging on an offer. This adds a very sour note to what should be a harmonious beginning of a lifelong adventure.

PART TWO

THE CAREER PATHS

5

Introduction to Anthropology Career Paths

Jane Goodall, famous for her work with chimpanzees, is an anthropologist.

Michael Crichton, author of *Jurassic Park*, was an anthropology major. The novelist Kurt Vonnegut studied anthropology.

Steve Riggio, chief executive officer of the Barnes and Noble bookstore chain, was an anthropology major.

John Collier, who as head of the U.S. Bureau of Indian Affairs was responsible for sweeping reforms in federal policy and relations with Indian tribes in the 1930s, was an anthropologist.

Singers Tracy Chapman and Mick Jagger also studied anthropology.

The first president of Kenya, Jomo Kenyatta, was an anthropology major. So was Prince Charles of England.

And the list goes on and on.

Anthropology provides students with valuable skills for a variety of professions. As you can see from the preceding roster, not all anthropology majors go on to study chimpanzees or little-known nomadic tribes. They write books, compose music, run businesses, influence government policy, and even lead countries.

In the pages that follow, you will learn about the countless options open to you with your anthropology degree. To fully understand those options, though, let's start with a brief review of the field of study itself.

The Paths of Study

Anthropology combines the biological, historical, physical, social, and earth sciences in a unique study of humankind. It is the only discipline that examines and attempts to understand humankind as a whole, by exploring biological and cultural characteristics of humans, past and present.

Anthropologists focus on the physical, social, and cultural development and behavior of humans. Their interests range from ancient to modern times, from the study of culture and social relations to human biology and evolution to language, the arts, and architecture.

The central issue in anthropology is human variation. It is global and comparative, studying human behavior across time and space and comparing those variations with each other. Its subject matter can be as provocative and exotic as coming-of-age practices in western Africa or as prosaic as the anatomy of the hand. Its focus can be as universal as human evolution or as focused as the use of handmade tools. Anthropologists may study ancient hieroglyphics or the corporate culture of a car manufacturer.

But there is a common thread that unites these different areas of study. Anthropologists are careful observers of humans and their behavior, and they strive to acquire knowledge of who we are and how we got to where we are.

Anthropologists may conduct their studies by examining archaeological remains, languages, or physical characteristics of people in different parts of the world.

Anthropologists often specialize in one or more geographic regions of the world—for example, Latin America, Eastern Europe, the Pacific Rim, or sub-Saharan Africa. With such firsthand experience around the world, anthropologists contribute to a pool of understanding about specific social and ethnic groups and about biological, ecological, and cultural factors that influence human behavior.

There are four main subfields of anthropology: archaeology, cultural (or social) anthropology, physical (or biological) anthropology, and linguistics. Each of the four subfields has its own skills, theories, and databases of special knowledge. Most anthropologists, therefore, pursue careers in only one of the four subdisciplines.

Archaeology
Archaeology can be defined as the study of past ways of life based on interpretation of material culture. Archaeologists focus on the material objects

made by past peoples and learn what they can about the beliefs and behavior of those people by examining those objects.

Scientific archaeological research includes excavating ancient sites. But modern archaeology doesn't depend on excavation alone. In fact, it frequently requires no excavation. Using modern methods of analysis, archaeologists look to existing collections in museums and information gathered previously to reinterpret them. Chapter 8 covers in-depth career opportunities in this popular field.

Cultural Anthropology

Cultural, or social, anthropology is the discipline's largest branch in North America. Cultural anthropologists seek to understand the internal workings of other societies, both primitive and complex. Although the traditional image is of the cultural anthropologist living in a hut in some remote jungle village, today cultural anthropologists also focus on groups closer to home, applying anthropological perspectives to their own culture and society. And while cultural anthropologists originally focused on a culture viewed as a whole, these days anthropologists might focus on just one aspect of life, such as religion, art, politics, folklore, witchcraft, symbolism, ecology, or astronomy.

Cultural anthropologists find careers in every facet of work life: federal, state, and local government; international agencies; health-care centers; non-profit associations; research institutes; and marketing firms as research directors, science analysts, and program officers.

Physical Anthropology

Physical, or biological, anthropologists study the evolution of the human body and our primate relatives. They observe biological behavior and attempt to understand ongoing human evolution. They also examine human adaptations to particular environments, such as the short- or long-term effects of high-altitude living.

Physical anthropology is the branch of the field with the most focus on natural science and, as a result, requires advanced training beyond a bachelor's degree. There are fewer jobs available for physical anthropologists than for cultural anthropologists, but this does not mean jobs don't exist. Professors sometimes look for qualified research assistants to work under a grant. Physical anthropologists who have an emphasis in the medical sciences, such as anatomy, biology, and organic chemistry, can pursue medical anthropology careers. Chapter 6 contains more information on related careers for physical anthropologists.

Linguistic Anthropology

Linguistic anthropology is one of the discipline's traditional, but small, branches. Linguistic anthropologists study the role of language in various cultures. They look at the history, evolution, and internal structure of human languages. They study links between different languages and try to explain the very nature of language itself. They find work in most of the same organizations that cultural anthropologists do: government agencies, private corporations, institutions of higher education, and nonprofit organizations.

There are also other subfields of study such as forensic, medical, business, educational, and developmental anthropology. These all have practical applications to the working world and are covered in Chapter 6.

As mentioned in the introduction to this book, the study of anthropology provides students with a wide base of skills useful in employment in a variety of professions. Each subfield provides similar as well as differing skills; it is helpful to know which skills you can acquire from which course of study and how those skills apply to the career you ultimately choose for yourself.

The Career Paths

Anthropology provides an excellent liberal arts background, which can be used in many careers. In general, anthropology majors find work in four broad sectors: education, government, nonprofit organizations, and private corporations. Other anthropology graduates use their training in the discipline as a foundation for work in other related fields.

Some positions require education beyond a bachelor's degree. A doctorate is required for most academic jobs, but more than a third of all anthropologists with Ph.D.s take jobs outside of the academic environment. A doctorate is also recommended for full professional status as an anthropologist, although work in museums, physical anthropology labs, field archaeology, and other settings, such as within the government and private sector, is often possible with a master's degree.

More and more, graduate students begin their training keeping academic as well as nonacademic careers in mind. They seek admission to programs with faculty who have experience in anthropology or nonacademic careers.

For the purpose of this book, we will examine four main career paths. These paths are in no way exhaustive; the list of main tracks numbers in the dozens. Within those tracks are dozens more job titles. Many are explored throughout the following four chapters, as primary paths or secondary and related paths.

The four paths are as outlined here:

- **Path 1: Creating Your Own Anthropology Career (Chapter 6).** This chapter covers medical anthropology, educational anthropology, business anthropology, working for the government, and private consulting, as well as several other anthropology careers. People working in these fields are called practicing anthropologists or applied anthropologists, as they work outside the academic community in "real-world" settings.
- **Path 2: Academic Careers (Chapter 7).** This chapter looks at the academic life and discusses options for teaching in secondary schools, two-year colleges, and four-year colleges and universities.
- **Path 3: Archaeology (Chapter 8).** This chapter covers the many different subfields of archaeology.
- **Path 4: Museums and Libraries (Chapter 9).** There is a wide range of job titles for anthropology majors choosing museum or library work. This chapter covers everything from curator to bibliographer.

Possible Job Settings

Here is a list of possible employers for anthropology majors:

Agency for International Development (AID)
Archives
Banks
Bureau of Land Management
Colleges and universities
Community arts organizations
Community development agencies
Consulting firms
Contract archaeology firms
Cultural agencies
Department of the Interior
Elementary and secondary schools

Ethnic agencies
Foreign aid agencies
Foreign Service
Foundations
Health-care agencies
Historic preservation offices
Historical societies
Hospitals
Immigrant organizations
International businesses
International health organizations
Law offices
Libraries
Medical centers
Medical schools
Migrant worker advocacy agencies
Minority advocacy agencies
Museums
National Institutes of Health
National Park Service
National Science Foundation
Nonprofit organizations
Pharmaceutical firms
Physical anthropology laboratories
Private corporations
Public education institutions
Public health centers
Research institutes and laboratories
Social service agencies
State transportation departments
United Nations
U.S. Forest Service
World Bank
World Health Organization
Zoos

Possible Job Titles

Many jobs filled by anthropologists don't mention the word *anthropologist* in the job announcement at all. The positions are broadly described to attract researchers, evaluators, and project managers. Anthropologists' unique training and skills enable them to compete successfully for these jobs.

You will find that job titles are as many and varied as the job settings just listed. However, the titles may reflect different responsibilities in different settings. For example, researchers work in labs, universities, private foundations, and government agencies, although the work they do in each setting might be quite different. Similarly, an educator working at a museum will have duties that differ from an educator working in a university. The job title you see advertised will not necessarily reveal the breadth and scope of the work involved; you will find these things out from other sources, such as job descriptions and face-to-face interviews.

The following list of job titles is meant as a guideline and is in no way exhaustive. Your own efforts at job hunting and job creating will no doubt let you add to the list.

Advertising campaign manager
Analyst
Applied anthropologist
Archaeologist
Archivist
Art director
Bilingual educator
Biological anthropologist
Conservator
Consultant
Counselor
Cultural anthropologist
Cultural resource manager
Curator
Diplomat
Director
Ecologist
Educator
Environmentalist
Forensic scientist
Fund-raiser
Genealogist
Health services provider
Historical archaeologist
Interpreter
Lawyer

Librarian
Linguistic anthropologist
Manager
Market researcher
Medical anthropologist
Museum exhibit designer
Museum registrar
Museum technician
Nurse practitioner
Park guide
Park ranger
Physical anthropologist
Physician
Planner
Police officer
Policy consultant
Practicing anthropologist
Product developer
Professor
Project evaluator
Registered nurse
Researcher
Service provider
Social anthropologist
Social worker
Teacher
Technical writer
Tour guide
Translator
Web designer

The Work Anthropologists Do

The actual work anthropologists do is limited only by the imagination. Here are just a few examples of projects in which anthropologists are involved. More are provided in the remaining chapters.

Some anthropologists study cultures and society. Some specialize in folklore and work in state and local historical societies or at community arts organizations. Others do fieldwork in other countries, studying different societies and cultures. They may record family and group relationships and activities or gather information on the behavior, language, and biology of different societies.

Some anthropologists work for government agencies. Archaeologists work for transportation departments, excavating sites before new highways are built. Forensic anthropologists work with police agencies to identify remains. Other anthropologists advise government departments and private organizations on the concerns of different peoples.

Anthropologists work to improve the health and welfare of many people. For example, they work in health agencies researching family-planning practices. They work for bioethics teams that provide ethics consultations to physicians and families. Cultural or social anthropologists examine the problems of teen pregnancy, urban crime, or domestic violence. They work on projects providing services to Native Americans or information and services to AIDS patients.

Anthropologists also work for a variety of businesses. They work with baby food manufacturers, studying infant feeding practices. They help car companies develop more comfortable seating. They work for large corporations, helping with employee relations. They work in the field of technology, helping to identify acceptance patterns of new technology both in the United States and abroad. They develop and test new ideas and products.

Anthropologists work in school or academic settings. They write and present research findings. They teach anthropology.

Wherever cross-cultural relations are involved, or wherever culturally broad perspectives are important, anthropologists make strong contributions.

Training and Qualifications

More than 350 U.S. colleges and universities offer an undergraduate major in anthropology, and many more offer course work. Many university programs allow for a great deal of latitude in designing majors and courses of study and it is now common practice to pursue interdisciplinary degrees. With a little bit of guidance and creativity, you should be able to make a case for your anthropology degree in any area you wish to enter.

Anthropology is not a large discipline. There are only about fifteen thousand anthropologists actively engaged in the profession. About six thousand bachelor's degrees are awarded in anthropology each year, as well as approximately one thousand master's degrees and four hundred doctorates.

The average time needed to complete an M.A. is two years and a Ph.D. about eight years. The time involved is due in part to the custom of completing a field project for the thesis or dissertation, which requires mastering several bodies of knowledge about the area—including comprehensive language training—before departing for the field site. Field research generally takes several months for the master's degree and from twelve to thirty months for the doctorate.

Most people employed as practicing anthropologists have an M.A. and/or a Ph.D., with a rapidly increasing number holding the master's degree. The required degree will vary depending on the expectations of employers, the region, the work setting, and your own skills.

Relatively few jobs outside of college teaching or anthropological museum work explicitly require a degree in anthropology. This means that for work outside those two areas, you will be competing with people holding various other degrees. Nevertheless, many master's-level candidates successfully compete for jobs in local, state, and federal agencies, as well as nonprofit organizations and private corporations.

Undergraduate anthropology majors, especially those interested in cultural anthropology, would do well to have some experience living overseas, either through a study-abroad program or through a two-year stint in the Peace Corps. Living abroad will make you appreciate cultural differences and will prepare you for doing fieldwork in another culture.

Dr. Sharlotte Neely, professor and coordinator of anthropology at Northern Kentucky University, offers this advice about preparing yourself for a career in anthropology:

"While many academic departments offer training that will help prepare you for careers in practicing (or applied) anthropology, there are numerous departments that offer programs that are specially designed to offer this kind of preparation at the M.A. and Ph.D. levels. These programs are characterized by more elaborate training in general social science methodology, good working relationships with academic programs in relevant cognate fields (e.g., medicine, education, agriculture, business, public health, nursing), faculty members who do practicing anthropology as a part of their academic work, and a strong commitment to internships and practicums. Programs offering career-oriented training at the M.A. level have been developed recently, often with special emphasis in a particular area of work such as public archaeology or medical anthropology. The considerable growth in the number of M.A. holders compared with the number of Ph.D. holders in anthropology in recent years reflects the success of M.A. training programs for practicing anthropology.

"Preparing for a career as a practicing anthropologist requires solid and well-rounded academic training. First, you should take available courses that will provide you with a strong grounding in anthropological theories, research methodologies, and analytical methods.

"Second, you should take courses that give you a broad exposure to anthropological work in particular topical areas (e.g., social organization, human migration, forensic sciences) and geographic areas of the world (e.g., the Middle East, Mexico).

"Third, identify your subfield of interest within the discipline (e.g., biological anthropology, linguistics, medical anthropology) and enroll in core courses within your subfield.

"Next, you should take courses offered in other departments that complement your core courses and coincide with your broad career interests (e.g., if your interest is biological anthropology, you might take courses in anatomy and physiology).

"Finally, it is important to get training in writing, statistics, computer analysis, qualitative data analysis, and public speaking. While proceeding through your curriculum, you will develop your conceptual and analytical abilities. Take advantage of extracurricular activities that will provide you with opportunities to increase your oral and written communication skills. Excellent interpersonal skills also are essential for a practicing anthropologist.

"When considering graduate school, apply only to universities that specialize in your interests (Indians of the Southwest, medical anthropology, hominid evolution, and so forth).

"Review the universities listed in the *AAA* [American Anthropological Association] *Guide* to departments of anthropology; talk with the anthropology faculty about your choices; visit the universities of your choice and make an appointment to meet with at least one member of the anthropology faculty. If you cannot visit, correspond with one of the professors in order to stand out from the crowd. Request information on scholarships, assistantships, fellowships, and other forms of financial help; apply to at least two universities; apply for admission at least nine months before you plan to start.

"Be aware of job prospects, and choose courses accordingly. Be well informed about job placement. Take time to build contacts with professionals outside your institution. Go to meetings and make contacts as early as possible. Make yourself highly visible. Don't overestimate your opportunities in the future job market. Find a niche that is not overpopulated."

Career Outlook

Anthropology majors seeking positions as pure social scientists can expect to encounter keen competition in certain areas of the field. The job market for academic anthropologists is relatively steady, but demand for anthropologists is increasing in other areas. The growth in nontraditional jobs for anthropologists is stimulated by an increasing need for good analysts and researchers, in positions where their data-gathering, communication, and quantitative skills can be put to good use.

Prospects for jobs are best for those holding advanced degrees, and often those positions are found in nonacademic settings. Government agencies; health and social service organizations; marketing, research, and consulting firms; and a wide range of businesses seek graduates with an anthropology background—or with skills that anthropology majors possess. Often, though, the job titles seem unrelated to the academic discipline.

While employment opportunities for practicing anthropologists are growing, locating these opportunities is not always easy. Chapter 6 will guide you as you create a career for yourself based on your anthropology degree.

Earnings

As a general rule, anthropologists working outside of a university setting earn more money than their campus counterparts. But salaries range widely, and several factors affect the pay level. These include the employer's estimate of your expertise based on your training and experience, the geographic location of the job, and the budget of the hiring organization. According to the Bureau of Labor Statistics, the average salary for an anthropologist is $41,800.

Anthropologists with a master's degree could start with entry-level salaries in the private sector of $25,000; M.A. holders with little or no experience working in local government or for a community organization might start out a little bit higher. Those working in large corporate settings or in medical settings can expect about $30,000 to start.

Most midcareer practicing anthropologists make $40,000 to $75,000 annually. At the upper end of the salary range, a small number of practicing anthropologists make in excess of $100,000 annually. Often yearly salaries are supplemented by royalties from publications and occasional consulting work.

Entry-level positions in college teaching in anthropology pay around $37,000 for the academic year. Beginning positions in anthropology with the federal government have pay that ranges from $26,000 with a B.A. to $35,500 with a master's degree. Positions in government for those with a doctorate in anthropology offer salaries in excess of $60,000.

Earnings in business and industry vary widely, but they are usually about 35 percent higher than in colleges and universities.

Working Conditions

Working conditions for anthropologists vary depending on the job setting, the location, and the nature of the organization for which they work. The organization's size, demographics, goals, and resources will all affect your role. If your job involves fieldwork overseas, you will be faced with a whole new set of conditions: a different standard of living; differing cultural values, laws, health services, and product availability; and work that requires physical exertion, just to name a few.

Some jobs, whether at home or overseas, present certain dangers and risks. Anthropologists studying urban gang behavior, for example, or the relationship between drug use and AIDS infection, might encounter dangerous situations requiring special skills in conflict resolution and building rapport.

Problems can also arise when anthropologists work with professionals from different academic and disciplinary backgrounds who have differing ideological approaches and methods. And those who follow a consulting or contract path could find that they must continually market their expertise to find new work once the contract or consulting term has expired.

The exceptions notwithstanding, most social scientists have regular hours. Those who don't participate in fieldwork usually work behind a desk, either alone or in collaboration with other social scientists. Those in a university setting usually divide their time among teaching, research and writing, consulting, and administrative responsibilities. Academic anthropologists might experience the pressures of writing and publishing articles, meeting deadlines, and adhering to tight schedules.

Specific conditions for each career path are discussed in the chapters ahead.

Strategies for Finding the Jobs

You can use many strategies to help you find the job you want. First, identify your skills and abilities that are related to your anthropological training, and pinpoint which job markets they match.

Next, realize that practicing anthropologists perform a wide range of job duties, such as research, program design and management, program evaluation, teaching, or training. Talk to friends and contacts who hold these positions to get a real sense of what each type of position involves.

Meanwhile, start amassing as much experience as you can during your academic years. Participate in internships and practicums, and volunteer whenever possible. These internships are very important because they help you get practical, hands-on experience. Try to participate in more than one internship, if possible, in different fields of the discipline, so you can get a mixed taste of what the careers have to offer.

Through your internships and volunteer experiences, you also build a network of contacts with people who may help you find work later. Employers prefer to hire people they know and have worked with. An internship can provide you with a foot in the door when an opening occurs.

Contact your school's department about arranging internships. If your department cannot help you, first decide what kind of work you would like to do, then contact the various organizations, government bodies, or institutions that do work in that area. To find these organizations, check with your library or contact the professional associations listed throughout this book.

When you are ready to apply for positions, consult a variety of sources for information about job opportunities. Check your university's placement center, your department's message board, newspaper ads, the *Chronicle of Higher Education*, the American Anthropological Association (AAA) website (see the "Resources" at the end of this chapter), and online job listings.

Remember that you will not often see job openings for an "anthropologist" outside of a university setting. Instead, you will see job titles such as intercultural trainer, program director, consultant, refugee services coordinator, policy scientist, curator, development officer, city planner, housing administrator, market analyst, archaeologist, project development officer, and others, for which your skills and work experience may qualify you.

Tailor your résumé to each job opening. (Part One of this book provides you with sample formats.) Then customize a cover letter to send out with your résumé, making sure you highlight your skills and abilities as they apply to the position for which you are applying. Both in the letter and during interviews, do not assume that an employer is knowledgeable about your unique perspective and training. Remember to provide employers with the details of your specific skills and abilities.

As you search for a job, remember to network. Contact people with whom you've worked and volunteered. Attend the AAA's annual conference, as employers also attend. The AAA's website, listed at the end of this chapter, gives more information.

Resources

American Anthropological Association
2200 Wilson Blvd., Suite 600
Arlington, VA 22201
aaanet.org

National Association for the Practice of Anthropology (NAPA)
American Anthropological Association
2200 Wilson Blvd., Suite 600
Arlington, VA 22201
practicinganthropology.org

National Association of Student Anthropologists (NASA)
American Anthropology Association
2200 Wilson Blvd., Suite 600
Arlington, VA 22201
aaanet.org/nasa/index.htm

Society for Applied Anthropology (SfAA)
P.O. Box 2436
Oklahoma City, OK 73101
sfaa.net

For information about careers in demography, contact:

Population Association of America
8630 Fenton St., Suite 722
Silver Spring, MD 20910
popassoc.org

Information about careers in sociology is available from:

American Sociological Association
1307 New York Ave. NW, Suite 700
Washington, DC 20005
asanet.org

6

Path I: Creating Your Own Anthropology Career

As you learned in Chapter 5, many jobs filled by anthropologists don't have the word *anthropologist* in the job announcement. Such jobs as researchers, evaluators, program directors, and project managers are positions that utilize the same skills that anthropology majors possess. Many employers, however, don't understand that anthropologists have the training and skills they are seeking and, therefore, don't specify someone with a degree in anthropology as the ideal job candidate. There are many job opportunities out there, all well suited to anthropology majors, but you will need to use your imagination and creativity to find these positions. If you look only for jobs specifically requesting anthropologists, you will limit the range of positions available to you.

"Anthropological training and experience are applicable in many work settings," Dr. Sharlotte Neely, anthropology professor at Northern Kentucky University, explains, "but require anthropologists to stretch the imagination to envision possibilities. To discover job opportunities that appeal to you, you will have to explore opportunities that do not sound like traditional anthropology. Your imagination will be a critical factor in finding these openings. You will need to be able to look at a situation and recognize the possibilities for anthropological skills, and then be able to help others recognize that fit. It is not enough to present yourself as an anthropologist and expect employers to realize that you have skills and approaches that they need. You will have to relate your experiences and education to situations that you might not think of as anthropology. You will have to learn how to adapt your language and the way in which you present yourself to others so that you can be seen and heard by potential employers."

"You need to be able to see an opportunity and say, 'Anthropological skills will work here.' They may not say, 'We need an anthropologist,'" confirms anthropologist Cathleen E. Crain, a managing partner in a growing consulting firm specializing in health and human services.

The remainder of this chapter gives you a bird's-eye view of scores of fields anthropology majors enter. It includes several firsthand accounts of other anthropology majors who are successfully using their skills in creative ways.

Definitions of the Career Paths

Let's first look at definitions for the terms *practicing anthropologist* and *applied anthropologist*. Some professionals consider the two terms to be synonymous. They define practicing or applied anthropologists as those who work outside of the academic community, in "real-world" situations such as private or non-profit corporations, government agencies, and various trade and business settings, whether full-time or on a consulting basis. They are "practicing" in their field or "applying" their skills to the world of nonacademic work.

Others define a practicing anthropologist as someone who works outside of the university setting and an applied anthropologist as someone whose primary work is within the academic community but who consults from time to time for corporations, government agencies, and various business settings. For the purposes of this book, we will consider the terms to be synonymous.

In the early 1970s, 88 percent of Ph.D. holders took jobs in traditional academic departments such as anthropology, sociology, biology, and ethnic studies. Today one-third of new doctors find professional jobs off-campus. In addition to archaeology and cultural resource management, museum and library work, and academic teaching and research, the main areas of employment are now business or corporate anthropology, medical anthropology, and social services within a variety of departments in the government.

Defining all of the areas of anthropology is even more difficult than deciding the correct usage of practicing versus applied anthropology. Reed Riner, professor of anthropology at Northern Arizona University in Flagstaff, says, "The last decade's set of convenient labels, such as Educational Anthropologist, Medical Anthropologist, or Business Anthropologist, may be stereotypic to the point of distortion in discussing where graduating applied anthropologists are getting hired. As our cohorts seem to demonstrate, the jobs, like the candidates, are one of a kind and are typically outside, or astride, what were 'conventional' categories named in the [19]80s.

"For example, an Educational Anthropologist could be defined as an anthropologist who works with educational issues or in an educational setting—and the same for Business Anthropology—with the dilemma that 'education' or 'business' can occur in almost any kind of circumstance."

The remainder of this section explores some definitions of the different fields, but again, keep in mind that this list is by no means exhaustive. In your own career research you will, no doubt, be able to add to the list.

Action Research Anthropology

For a definition of this interesting line of work, turn to *Applied Anthropology, An Introduction* by John van Willigen (2002). The author says research occurs "when individuals of a community join together with a professional researcher to study and transform their community in ways they mutually value." In this mode, "the anthropologist works with the community to understand the conditions that produce the problems that the people face. . . . The applied anthropologist becomes an auxiliary to the naturally occurring community leadership." Working in conjunction with community leaders, the action anthroplogist works to identify potential solutions to community problems.

Organizational Anthropology

The term *organizational anthropology* is often used instead of the individual terms of *business*, *corporate*, or *industrial anthropology*. These terms all refer to the anthropological study and analysis of organizations in the public, private, for-profit, and nonprofit domains.

Anthropologists in the business world work in advertising, market development, business management, economic development, government, health care, and many other areas. The private sector often provides the chance to work as part of multidisciplinary teams, both within organizations and in the field. For example, a corporate anthropologist working in market research might conduct targeted focus groups to examine consumer preference patterns not readily apparent through statistical or survey methods.

Consulting

Consultants usually have a Ph.D. along with significant experience. A Ph.D. is particularly important for work as a consultant in international development settings or in medical institutions. In addition to your degree, your particular skills and experience play a critical part in the hiring process.

Consultants' work might include historical and ethnographic research for Indian tribes; forensic work for police agencies; archaeological survey and excavation; social and cultural impact assessments for large-scale construction projects; bilingual and bicultural curricula design with school professionals; or health-care services assessments for specific cultural groups.

Survey results shed some light on the number of anthropologists working in the consulting field. In the 1990 National Association of Practicing Anthropologists Membership Survey (the most recent available), 25 percent of the respondents indicated that they worked in the private sector for consulting firms, as independent consultants, or in corporations. According to the 1990 American Anthropological Association (AAA) survey of anthropology Ph.D.s, 8 percent of respondents listed themselves as employed in consulting firms or as self-employed. The proportion of consultants in the NAPA survey is higher because the organization is oriented toward anthropological practice, and its membership (and thus its survey) is not limited to Ph.D. holders but includes bachelor's and master's degree holders as well.

Consulting work generally falls into two categories. The first consists of self-employed, full-time independent consultants (freelancers), part-time consultants, and people involved in small, privately owned companies. They usually find consulting work by bidding on publicly announced contracts, by publicizing their services to community organizations, provider institutions, companies, and government agencies, and by networking with key people in organizations in their area of specialization.

The keys to success for freelancers and small consulting firm owners are becoming well known and developing a track record. Getting started might involve a considerable amount of time soliciting new work, but once you're established, new opportunities can come quickly.

The second category of consulting work includes anthropologists who are employees of large contract research companies or midsize consulting companies. Often anthropologists in these organizations specialize in a certain field, such as healthcare, international development, organizational management, or natural resources. Anthropologists in larger firms do not have to hunt down contracts, but they may have less control over the work assignments they are asked to take on.

Some examples of consulting jobs filled by anthropologists include:

- A senior consultant in an organizational management consulting firm
- A vice president of a small consulting firm that specializes in natural resource management
- An independent consultant based in Kenya who specializes in public health and family planning
- An anthropologist who works in the agricultural and natural resource division of a large, Washington, D.C.–based consulting firm that focuses on international development work

- A president of a consulting firm that specializes in cultural resource management and archaeology
- A part-time independent consultant who specializes in program development, organizational technical assistance, evaluation, and grant writing for community-based health, arts, and social service organizations

Educational Anthropology

As mentioned earlier, "education" can take place in any number of settings—museums, hospitals, clinics, social service agencies, private corporations, and so on. Anthropologists can make a case for their ability to teach for a variety of employers.

Forensic Anthropology

Forensic anthropologists work with police departments to help identify mysterious or unknown remains. They also work in university and museum settings.

Government

Anthropologists are strongly represented in every aspect of the local, state, and federal government. Anthropologists can currently be found in such widely diverse agencies as:

Agency for International Development (AID)
Bureau of Indian Affairs
Bureau of Land Management
Bureau of Reclamation
Bureau of the Census
Centers for Disease Control
Defense Language Institute
Department of Agriculture
Department of Education
Department of Housing and Urban Development
Department of the Interior
Government Accounting Office
Health Resources and Services Administration
National Cancer Institute
National Institutes of Health
National Oceanic and Atmospheric Administration
National Park Service
National Science Foundation

Office of Bilingual Education
Peace Corps
Smithsonian Institution
State and local historical societies
State parks departments
State transportation departments
U.S. Army Central Identification Laboratory
U.S. Army Corps of Engineers
U.S. Environmental Protection Agency
U.S. Forest Service
U.S. Indian Health Service
U.S. Soil Conservation Service

Anthropologists work in these departments and agencies as evaluators, managers, planners, program directors, research analysts, service providers, and policy makers. Some are also employed as staff members for congressional committees. Most government positions require a master's degree.

The federal government also hires archaeologists holding bachelor's degrees for cultural resource management–related work. You can read more about this area in Chapter 8.

Medical Anthropology

Medical anthropologists study environmental and sociocultural factors in disease and disability and apply anthropological theory and methods to understand human health issues. Research in this field addresses, for example, problems in health care among ethnic communities; age groups at special risk; and populations undergoing change, such as refugees and immigrants.

Biological and medical anthropologists have valuable skills that are useful in the growing sector of health-related occupations.

Dr. Richard Meindl, professor and chair of the Department of Anthropology at Kent State University, says, "Probably the most important field outside of university teaching (it is actually close to university teaching) is the field of anatomy. Medical schools tend to prefer biological anthropologists to other professionals in biomedical sciences because some anthro programs emphasize human gross anatomy.

"There are opportunities in technical programs such as occupational therapy and in physical therapy, but only for those anthropologists who can teach gross anatomy, especially appendicular anatomy (limbs) and head and neck."

Social Services and Nonprofit Organizations

Anthropologists have the skills to enter a variety of social service fields, working as social workers, researchers, educators, and program directors, and studying such problems as urban crime, HIV, teen pregnancy, and gang behavior. Agencies such as Catholic Relief Services, the Christian Children's Fund, American Friends Service Committee, International Red Cross, World Health Organization, and various local, state, and government agencies are examples of employers in the social services.

Sample Job Listings

The following sample job listings will give you an idea of the range of jobs available. Because these positions have already been filled, the names of the hiring body and contact information have been deleted.

Project Coordinator, Drug Monitoring Study. The study employs ethnographic and survey methods to research current and changing drug use patterns in an inner-city area. The project coordinator is responsible for supervising an ethnographer, an evaluator, two outreach workers, and student interns; conducting literature reviews and tracking drug trends on the Internet; serving as liaison for a community advisory board; and writing, presenting, and publishing findings. Qualifications: Ph.D. preferred or M.A. plus research experience. Bilingual (Spanish-English) a plus.

Research Assistant. With funding from the Centers for Disease Control, the organization is conducting a survey designed to learn about factors related to HIV/AIDS among black men who have sex with men and what can be done to prevent HIV in this community. Conduct interviews and assist with coordination of focus groups; code and clean data; assist with data analysis; conduct library and Internet research; and assist with the preparation of reports and publications.

Work Anthropologist. Corporation seeks candidate with expertise in the anthropology of work, ethnographic research, and data synthesis and analysis. The person in this position will be a member of a customer-centered innovation

---

continued

team that conceives, prototypes, and assesses the value of new product concepts and how they fit into existing work practices. The position requires a Ph.D./M.A. in anthropology, with an emphasis on cognitive psychology and linguistics. Demonstrated experience working in field sites and on project teams required. Experience in observational techniques, participant-observation, interview techniques, and ethnographic analysis required.

Programs

In addition to the many universities that offer traditional graduate programs in anthropology, a smaller number have special master's degree programs in applied anthropology.

Graduate Programs

The following is a partial list of schools that offer graduate programs in applied anthropology. A more complete list can be found in the *AAA Guide*, available from the American Anthropological Association, or by subscription online as the AAA E-Guide.

Boston University
California State University–Chico
California State University–Long Beach
Florida State University
Georgia State University
Michigan State University
Northern Arizona University
Oregon State University
State University of New York–Binghamton
State University of New York–Buffalo
University of Connecticut
University of Kansas
University of Miami
University of Maryland

Sample Master's Programs

The following two university programs offer a master of arts in applied anthropology. The first, at Boston University, offers a program geared toward students with an undergraduate major in a field other than anthropology. The second, at the University of Maryland, is open only to students who have a bachelor's in anthropology.

Boston University

"The applied anthropology master's program is designed for nonanthropologists who are already engaged in, or plan to enter, such fields as medicine, public health, education, journalism, law, environmental management, social services to refugee or immigrant populations, rural development, or public policy evaluation. It is designed to provide the student with basic anthropological training and an appreciation of the significance of a cross-cultural perspective in professional practice. The master's degree is neither required nor encouraged as a stepping-stone to the Ph.D. Anyone intending to become a professional anthropologist should apply directly to the Ph.D. program.

"Applicants must have obtained a degree in some discipline other than anthropology and have an expressed intention to continue working in, or enter, that field. Prospective students should also explain in their written statements how they expect anthropology to enhance their capability or improve their effectiveness in their chosen career. This is important because students who enter the program with well-defined goals derive the most benefit from the resources that the department and the university have to offer.

"Students enrolled in the program must successfully complete a minimum of eight semester courses (thirty-two credits), two of which may be taken outside of the Department of Anthropology. During the first semester, the program coordinator assists students in choosing appropriate courses. By the second semester, students must select a major adviser from among the faculty. During their last semester, students may enroll in a directed study course under the guidance of their major adviser and begin developing a topic for the required research paper. While it is possible for a full-time student to fulfill all the program's requirements in two semesters, many students often need an extra semester of residency to fully complete their studies.

"The candidate must show proficiency in French, Spanish, German, or another language approved by the student's adviser or the graduate committee of the department. Certification is based on completing at least four semesters of course work in the language at the undergraduate level or passing a two-hour written comprehensive examination.

"Each student must write a special research paper under the direction of the major adviser and two other faculty members, one of whom may be from another department. The paper should demonstrate the candidate's ability to integrate anthropology with his or her own discipline or profession. It should be well conceived but modest in scope and can be based on either library or field research."

University of Maryland

The master's in applied anthropology is a forty-two-credit program, built around a central internship: all course work frames and supports the internship experience. There are four tracks: Applied Biological Anthropology, Community Health and Development, Historical Archaeology, and Resource Management and Cultural Process. The program provides an even balance between a practical internship experience and a solid academic foundation.

An undergraduate degree in anthropology is preferred, so no general anthropology is offered as a part of the M.A.A. curriculum: all core courses focus on application.

The internship is taken in the middle of the academic program: students prepare for the internship with applied anthropology course work and continue academic work in a related field after they have gained the practical experience of an internship.

This program promotes an entrepreneurial approach to nonacademic careers. Program flexibility encourages students to pursue individual interests and create their own niches.

This program does not require a thesis: students prepare a postinternship project, determined in consultation with faculty and dictated by the needs of the agency sponsoring the internship.

Close-Ups

The following firsthand accounts from practicing anthropologists show how they are using their degrees and skills in a variety of interesting work settings. Their work often defies categorization, other than placing them within the broad categories of private corporations or nonprofit organizations. You'll see what degrees they hold, the type of work they do, and in most cases, how they got started and what remuneration one can expect. They also offer valuable advice for people who are just starting out. What better way to learn how to create your own job than from other professionals who did just that?

Sharon Hodges—Organizational Anthropologist

Sharon Hodges works in the Department of Child and Family Studies at the Louis de la Parte Florida Mental Health Institute (FMHI), a research and training center for children's mental health at the University of South Florida. She earned her bachelor's degree in economics in 1975 at the University of

Florida; her master's of business administration in 1981 at the University of South Florida; and her Ph.D. in applied (cultural) anthropology in 1997, also at the University of South Florida.

Getting Started. "My background was in business management and included business consulting as well as teaching management in the USF College of Business. Anthropology offered fresh insight into the management of complex organizations. I began my work at FMHI as a graduate assistant and was later brought on as full-time staff.

"My early education and experience in business contribute considerably to my work, but I was hired as an applied anthropologist. My course work in theory and method of applied anthropology, fieldwork experience while I was in school, as well as my experience on research and technical assistance teams at FMHI have all contributed to my training."

The Realities of the Job. "I am an organizational anthropologist. My work is in human services (children's mental health) and includes work with public and private organizations.

"Although I am university-based, our work is focused on applied research and technical assistance with agencies and organizations that provide children's services, rather than classroom teaching.

"At FMHI we work with managers and administrators, direct service providers, and family members in human service systems (mental health, education, juvenile justice, and child welfare) that serve children with serious emotional disturbances and their families.

"Human services are very often delivered by large and complex organizations; hence the focus on organizational anthropology. I often explain what an anthropologist is doing in children's mental health by defining anthropology as the study of human behavior in a group setting.

"I love my work. It is extremely interesting. I meet wonderfully dedicated people involved in difficult work. Most of my work revolves around helping people figure out how we can do a better job providing services for children and families.

"Specifically, my work is about how to measure the results of service delivery. How do systems or agencies know if the children and families who receive services benefit from them, and how do they use that information to improve their planning and delivery of services?

"My work is a combination of fieldwork and office work. In the field, I rely primarily on qualitative methods such as (but not limited to) interviews, direct observation, document review, and focus groups to collect data around a specific research question. Often these questions result from problems identified by people within the child-serving agencies I am working with.

"In the office, my work involves a lot of reading, analysis, and writing. Because this is applied research, we work under tight deadlines to provide feedback from our field visits to the child-serving agencies. Sometimes this is written feedback, in the form of a report, and sometimes it is oral feedback that is part of a debriefing session with the agency.

"Most of my work is done on multidisciplinary research teams. This is a mental health institute, so there are a lot of psychologists on staff. But our teams are purposefully structured to include multiple-disciplinary perspectives. So in addition to psychologists, I often work on teams with social workers, educators, nurses, public administrators, and other anthropologists. On these teams, we design the research, collect and analyze the data, and write up the results. Sometimes I am in the role of project director, and sometimes I work as a team member.

"In addition to providing feedback to the sites where we conduct research, we are involved in broader dissemination of our results. We provide technical assistance to other child-serving agencies that make use of what we have learned in our research; we teach workshops, present at conferences, and write articles and chapters for journals and books.

"My workweek varies depending on my involvements. In the field, the days are long and the work, although always interesting, can be grueling. In the office, facing a deadline, the workweek can also be long. My workweek is almost always more than forty hours, although my time is somewhat flexible. This includes the ability to work at home some when I am on a writing deadline and to shift my schedule to early morning or late evening as meets my needs."

Earnings. "Beginning salaries at the Ph.D. level are about $40,000 a year. People with more experience or administrative/managerial responsibility earn around $80,000 a year. Top administrators (deans, department chairs) earn more than this."

Advice from Sharon Hodges. "Gain as much and as varied experience as possible. In applied work, that is invaluable. My work (and marketability) as an anthropologist is greatly enhanced by my experience in management. The catch-22 in applied work is that we are almost always applying anthropology in a field other than our own. This means it is very important to build skills and expertise outside of anthropology as well as within. It may also be an advantage to work in between working toward your degrees, as a strategy for gaining experience. I'm guessing I'm much more marketable with my long and varied work experience than a Ph.D. who went straight through school in ten years. Also, you have to be able to write and speak in public—and it helps to enjoy doing so."

Gordon Bronitsky—Consultant

Gordon Bronitsky is president of Bronitsky and Associates, a consulting and marketing firm in Albuquerque. He earned his bachelor's degree in anthropology from the University of New Mexico in 1971. At the University of Arizona he earned his master's and doctorate, both in anthropology, with a concentration in archaeology.

Getting Started. "Growing up, I thought anthropology and archaeology were the most interesting and fascinating subjects to read about. I wanted to be an anthropologist/archaeologist since I was twelve."

The Realities of the Job. "I work with American Indians in the United States, Canada, and Mexico doing international cultural marketing of traditional/contemporary art, music, dance; fashion; film/video; photography; theater; speakers and writers (native languages and English); food products; and Indian-owned tourism. My associates and I work as agents, brokers, promoters, grant writers, workshop leaders—anything the client requires.

"I go overseas with my clients when there is sufficient funding and they want me to go with them. We offer a broad range of talent and product and find buyers, venues, and exhibition space overseas. When I am overseas, I usually serve as a manager, making sure everything is OK with sites, lodging, transportation, and so on, and I help in sightseeing, too.

"Each day is different, especially since I can't predict when something will come up that has to be dealt with quickly, and my routine when I'm on the road with Indian clients overseas is totally different from my routine in the United States. The range goes something like this: I might have to locate and contact Indian food producers, for example, or find out the director of European marketing for the Pequot Foxwoods Resort, or call a dance group to find out if they have gotten their passports yet, or if they'll need a permit to bring eagle feathers into another country.

"What I like most is the pleasure of working with talented, passionate people, the honor that comes when people refer a relative to me or tell me that their art or music is the best they can do—and can I help them take it further.

"I like least the financial insecurity that goes with the territory, and persistent, ongoing white paternalism, which is best expressed in the surprise that Indian people want to be paid for what they do, and the ignorance that asserts itself in the belief that all that Indian people have to offer is beads, powwows, and feathers."

Advice from Gordon Bronitsky. "I would advise you to be sure this is what you want to do, to be sure you love it and that you are consumed with passion for it. You'll need a high threshold for frustration and uncertainty, and a low threshold for shoddy work and lack of talent."

Cris Johnsrud—Director of Research and Program Development

Cris Johnsrud owns a consulting firm called Pathfinder Research. Before founding her firm, she worked for more than fifteen years for the Southern Technology Applications Center (STAC), a technology transfer center based at the College of Engineering at the University of Florida.

She earned her bachelor's degree and master's, both in anthropology, at the University of Nebraska. She earned her Ph.D. in cultural anthropology at the University of Florida in 1989.

Getting Started. "I taught anthropology as a full-time faculty member at Des Moines Area Community College in Iowa, from 1975 to 1982. My experiences in working with a diverse student and faculty population and experience gained as chair of the curriculum revision committee provided a good base for subsequent program development responsibilities.

"I was attracted to archaeology as a youngster when I read books about the discovery of such things as the city of Troy, tombs of the Egyptian pharaohs, and other 'lost' treasures. To me it seemed quite romantic and exciting with a dash of mystery and detective work—many of the same attributes that made Indiana Jones such a popular icon.

"As a college student, I pursued archaeology but discovered that my interests had shifted. As a graduate student, I worked with a political anthropologist who had done significant research on peasants in Switzerland. Through her guidance, I began to realize that anthropological studies of contemporary Western society were tremendously fascinating, particularly the activities involved in the introduction of new technologies to traditional ways of doing things."

The Realities of the Job. "At STAC I was primarily a manager. Even though STAC is located in an academic institution and bound by the university's rules and regulations, it derives its funding and support from federal grants and contracts as well as from organizations who pay fees for work performed on their behalf. Thus, STAC operates much like a private-sector firm in the sense that they must follow the bottom line.

"I did not teach at the university, other than to give the occasional lecture on campus at someone's invitation. I did, however, work with students. These were mostly graduate students (M.B.A., engineering, one or two social science types) who were hired part-time for project work at STAC or on an internship basis.

"I truly loved working with graduate students, and I felt I learned as much from them as they did from me. They assisted us in a variety of projects, including researching the various ways new technology might be used in industry; helping universities and companies in deciding whether or not to patent a new technology; researching 'best practices' on a variety of topics, such as managing intellectual property; helping firms locate technologies they need to improve or expand products; helping federal laboratories to market to the private sector the technologies developed as part of their normal operations; or providing services via small-business incubators to help the entrepreneur or start-up owner build a viable company.

"It was my job to secure federal grants and contracts that enabled us to provide these services. Thus, I wrote a lot of proposals, mostly as responses to 'requests for proposal' (RFP). Prior to developing the actual proposals, I participated in a significant amount of strategic planning, information gathering on federal agencies and their funding priorities, new opportunities, and current events so we could develop proposals that not only were responsive but also showed that STAC was totally 'tuned in' to the funding agency's needs and was the best organization to help meet those needs.

"Along the way, I also tried to keep my associations and networks among anthropologists working—especially since I benefit so much from being able to talk with people who speak my 'language.' My training in ethnographic analysis and participant-observation was invaluable to me in developing plans and strategies for the organization and suggesting solutions to problems and questions for our many and varied client organizations."

Earnings. "I earned $60,000 a year plus benefits. What someone just starting out can expect to earn is totally dependent on the average salaries of the field/industry of interest. Because the Center I worked for is in the college of engineering, the starting salaries were reasonable. However, they initially suggested that my starting salary should be the equivalent of a starting salary in anthropology (then about $25,000 to $30,000). I insisted that I needed to be started at the equivalent of an engineering assistant professor's salary—more like $40,000 to $45,000—and that's what they did.

"Unlike the private sector where one can start at a relatively low salary and then leapfrog into higher brackets through bonuses, profit sharing, and generous raises, academic institutions and government agencies are controlled bureaucracies. That means that at whatever level you enter, your future earnings will be determined by low, lockstep raises."

Advice from Cris Johnsrud. "Anthropology students need to get as much education and experience as possible in nonanthropological areas—particularly areas in which they think they might like to develop careers. This includes business settings, working part-time in hospitals, or volunteering in neighborhood clinics or community development projects.

"Anthropology provides a powerful perspective and one of the most effective backgrounds an individual can have. But unless it is combined with outside experience, it is not particularly valued as an educational background by potential employers.

"Also, get experience in working with teams, if at all possible. Too often anthropology graduates have absorbed the individualistic perspectives necessary to survive and advance in an academic career (single-authored papers, single control of research projects, etc.), but this perspective carries with it a 'non-team-player' attitude in corporate and government arenas.

"Most people I know have built a career for themselves by being entrepreneurial within an organization—that is, being open to new opportunities. One technique is to say, 'I want to be involved in project X.' Chances are if they are successful, they will have established themselves as an integral part of the organization in the process. The next time project X or something similar comes around, people will more readily assume that the anthropologist who did it before must be the expert and so should be part of the team.

"Develop networks of contacts in a broad range of organizations, sectors, and settings. They can help in opening the doors to opportunities for jobs and involvement in various career-building projects.

"Academic professionals have a poor reputation outside of the Academy, largely due to an attitude that is perceived as 'know it all.' To work effectively in an organization, you need an attitude that says, 'I'm here to learn, to participate, to do what I'm asked to do to the best of my ability.'"

Bryan Byrne—Design Anthropologist

Bryan Byrne is involved in exciting new work for anthropologists, forming a consulting firm in product development. He earned his B.A. in 1985 at Beloit College, majoring in anthropology. His M.A. is in applied anthropology with a minor in environmental engineering, earned in 1990 from the University of Florida. In 1996 he earned his Ph.D., also from the University of Florida, with a concentration in sociocultural anthropology.

Getting Started. "My father is a retired anthropologist who taught at colleges in the Chicago area. I was in the womb when my parents were digging at Cahokia Mounds (an important archaeological site).

"At graduate school at the University of Florida I studied environmental engineering, biological evolution, nutritional anthropology, economic theory and history, ethnoarchaeology, social organization and kinship, applied anthropology, and so forth.

"I did a short internship in Washington, D.C., on a project funded by the UN about the consequences of atmospheric pollution by Western corporations, and I did my dissertation on the evolution of water management systems.

"On my travels through airports, I found several articles in Forbes and other business magazines about team-based approaches to creating new products. The idea stuck with me.

"After graduation in 1996, I quickly found out that few schools would consider me for a job. The international water development market was saturated, too. I struck out with all of the major managerial consulting firms, but then remembered speaking with Sue Squires at an NAPA meeting. I found that she worked with a product design firm. I told her that I'd been interested in the kind of work she was doing. Good timing: she was looking for an intern."

The Realities of the Job. "You may be interested in the work being conducted by a small group of anthropologists in the product development industry. Let's call it design anthropology. It's as good a name as any; since the field is so young, it really has no name.

"Basically, what we do is use our anthropological concepts and methods to help manufacturers and product designers invent, design, and evaluate products, services, distribution channels, development processes, marketing messages, computer interface processes, and even business strategy. If engineers are focused on the thing itself, and designers on the form of the thing itself, and business administrators on the means to make it profitable, then anthropologists try to make it fit with the needs, understandings, and behavior patterns of the businesses, marketers, retailers, purchasers, and consumers themselves. Consider this the corporate equivalent of 'appropriate technology.'

"Typically, anthropologists in this field work for small design and marketing consultancies, although some are employed by major manufacturers, research and design companies, and technology transfer companies. For example, I know of anthropologists working for Intel, Apple, Microsoft, Citicorp, Hallmark, and U.S. West. Others work for major research and development (R&D) firms such as Battelle, Xerox PARC, and the Global Business Network.

"At the moment, these people are just beginning to compare notes. Sue Squires and I coedited a book with anthropologists from some of these companies, entitled *Creating Breakthrough Ideas: The Collaboration of Anthropologists and Designers in the Product Development Industry* (2002).

"The work itself is well placed to make some sound theoretical and methodological contributions to anthropology. Not only does it require a knowledge of the principles uniting the four fields, but it also demands that anthropologists collaborate with engineers, architects, industrial designers, computer technicians, venture capitalists, managers, and consumers representing every industry and consumer niche.

"For example, ethnoarchaeology is useful because it tries to describe and analyze the interactions of people with regard to objects. The work we do requires us to pay close attention to current living situations, task goals, the functions of the product or service, and the means by which the consumer can understand them."

Earnings. "Consultants can generally start out at about $40 to $50 an hour, but they receive no benefits and cannot rely on a steady stream of contracts. Those with good business connections can boost their rates to $100 an hour. Once they get very good and have a proven reputation within the industry, they can charge up to $250 an hour. One rule is never accept a lower rate than you accepted for the last project you worked on."

Advice from Bryan Byrne. "Students who are interested in working in this field would be wise to study the following:

Ethnographic field research (interviews, video, experimental, participant-observation, literature review)
Project design

Analytical techniques (both qualitative and quantitative)
Ethnoarchaeology
Economics
Anthropological economics
Social organizations (describe, compare, and change)

Other courses:

Physics (basic)
Mechanical, electrical, and software engineering
Industrial design
Materials science
Business finance and accounting
Business management
Project management
Public speaking
Introduction to law (especially corporate and intellectual
    property)
Computer skills (text, qualitative search engines, accounting and
    bookkeeping, Internet, PowerPoint, etc.)
Languages: Spanish, Japanese, Mandarin

"It also helps to become knowledgeable about an industry or product range: computers, educational products, personal hygiene, health/medical, household products, and so forth.

"You have to learn how to use both inductive and deductive reasoning skills, write and communicate concisely, manage strong egos, multitask, create organizations, and ply your anthropological talents on rapid-fire projects.

"In general, the work is both thrilling and maddening. It's a process of continual discovery about many things in the world. That should suit anthropologists who are helplessly curious and can't stand routines composed of simple repetitive tasks."

Nadine Bendycki—Health-Care Marketing Consultant

Nadine Bendycki has been employed in health-care program development and marketing for more than twenty years. Currently, she is the founder and principal of MarketWhys, a consulting firm that specializes in health-care marketing, communications, and program development and evaluation. She earned her B.A. in anthropology in 1978 and her M.A. in cultural anthropology in 1979, both from Case Western Reserve University.

Getting Started. "I was applying for a position as a research assistant for a community-based health education program in the inner city. I cited my training in anthropology as relevant because I knew that the needs of the inner-city physicians as far as continuing education was concerned could differ substantially from the educational needs of university-based physicians. I talked about how anthropology helps you to examine the same objective situation from multiple perspectives. I also remember discussing how patients without money and education might be making rational choices about their health-care-seeking behavior, even if the professional did not understand or share the patients' rationale.

The Realities of the Job. "Many times large institutions are internally focused and do not explicitly keep the needs of the end user or the market in mind. My job as a health-care marketer is to keep this from happening by 'getting closer to the customer.'

"I also use my anthropology training to guide my applied business research; that is, using qualitative research to put flesh on the bones of the quantitative research that hospitals conduct to keep abreast of market developments, threats, and opportunities."

Advice from Nadine Bendycki. "Be yourself! Be enthusiastic! Be creative! Provide examples of where your training and experience in qualitative/anthropological methods would enhance the position you are seeking.

"Network with other anthropologists who apply their knowledge as well as with professionals in your specific area of expertise or interest (health care, marketing, bioethics, etc.).

"Gain practical experience through internships. Define your skill set (i.e., not what you know; what you can do with what you know). Improve and enhance your computer skills, such as word processing, spreadsheet, presentation graphics, database, HTML, Web design, and Web research.

"Get a professional mentor. Study and understand the organizational culture for each job you are applying for."

Strategies for Finding the Jobs

A variety of skills and resources will help you search out—or create—job opportunities.

Networking

Anthropologists traditionally use interpersonal networks to find jobs. In planning a career as a practicing anthropologist, you will need to cultivate networks with other practicing anthropologists. Getting involved in the NAPA Mentor Program, a service available to students who are interested in the field, is one of the many ways to begin this process. In this program, students are paired with practicing anthropologists. Their interaction may take many forms, including telephone conversations or face-to-face meetings to discuss internships, the job search, or career issues generally. For further information, go to NAPA's website at practicinganthropology.org/training and click on "Find a Mentor."

Internships

Internships prepare you for the world of work, provide references that will be invaluable in finding your first full-time job, and sometimes turn into permanent positions.

Membership in Professional Associations

The names and addresses of associations for every aspect of anthropology work are provided for you at the end of each chapter in Part Two of this book. Among other things, professional associations can keep you abreast of developments in your field, provide a network of contacts for you, and help you in your job search.

Identifying Your Skills

The importance of identifying your skills and communicating them to prospective employers and contacts can't be emphasized enough. Be open to jobs that do not come with the title of "anthropologist." The job title is not what's important. What you need to stress is what you can do, such as interviewing, directing, organizing, and so on. Make sure to translate your skills into terminology that will be meaningful to potential employers. Find out what they are seeking, and then make sure they know that you can provide it.

Resources

American Anthropological Association
2200 Wilson Blvd., Suite 600
Arlington, VA 22201
aaanet.org

The Association has more than a dozen specialized sections or interest groups, including the Biological Anthropology Section, the American Ethnological Society, the Council for Museum Anthropology, the Council on Nutritional Anthropology, the National Association of Practicing Anthropologists, the National Association of Student Anthropologists, the Society for the Anthropology of Work, and the Society for Medical Anthropology. For a complete list, go to aaanet.org/sctigs.htm.

American Association of Physical Anthropologists
P.O. Box 1897
Lawrence, KS 66044
physanth.org

Society for Applied Anthropology (SfAA)
P.O. Box 2436
Oklahoma City, OK 73101
sfaa.net

Washington Association of Professional Anthropologists
P.O. Box 23262, L'Enfant Plaza
Washington, DC 20026
smcm.edu/wapa

7

Path 2: Academic Careers

Teaching is the career path of choice for many people who feel that their love of and depth of knowledge in the subject area is best expressed by sharing it and developing it in others.

No matter which subfield of anthropology to be taught—archaeology, cultural, physical, or linguistic—all teachers must possess certain qualities and skills. Being knowledgeable about their subject; having the ability to communicate, inspire confidence, and motivate students; and understanding students' educational and emotional needs are all essential for teachers. They also should be organized, patient, and creative.

Definition of the Career Path

Anthropologists in educational settings teach classes and conduct research. They spend their time preparing for classes, writing lectures, grading papers, working with individual students, researching special interest topics and composing scholarly articles on their findings, and writing longer monographs and books for the general public or textbooks for their students.

To understand fully the career path, though, we first must look at the role of a teacher. This role is changing from that of a lecturer or presenter to one of a facilitator or coach. Interactive discussions and hands-on learning are replacing rote memorization. For example, rather than telling students about archaeology or physical anthropology, a teacher might ask students to perform a laboratory experiment or to conduct a survey and then discuss how the results apply to the real world.

As teachers move away from the traditional repetitive-drill approaches, they are using more props or manipulatives to help students understand abstract concepts, solve problems, and develop critical thinking processes. Classes are becoming less structured, and students are working in groups to discuss and solve problems together. Preparing students for the workforce is the major stimulus generating the changes in education. Employers today require their employees to interact with others, to adapt to new technology, and to logically think through problems. Teachers provide the tools and environment for their students to develop these skills.

Secondary Education

Secondary school teachers help students delve more deeply into subjects introduced in elementary school and learn more about the world and about themselves. They specialize in a specific subject, such as history, Spanish, or art.

Teachers may use technology in teaching. Computers are used in many classroom activities, from helping students solve math problems to learning English as a second language. The Internet can bring the real world into the classroom, for example, by allowing students to share personal experiences or research projects of interest with students in other countries. Teachers must continually update their skills to use the latest technology in the classroom.

Teachers design their classroom presentations to meet student needs and abilities. They also may work with students individually. Teachers assign lessons, give tests, hear oral presentations, and maintain classroom discipline. Teachers observe and evaluate a student's performance and potential. Increasingly, teachers are using new assessment methods, such as examining a notebook of a student's research project, to measure student achievement. At the end of a learning period, teachers assess students' overall progress. They may then provide additional assistance in areas where students need help.

College and University Teaching

College and university faculty teach and advise more than fourteen million full-time and part-time college students and play a significant role in our nation's research. They also meet with colleagues and study to keep up with developments in their field as well as consult with government, business, nonprofit, and community organizations.

Faculty members are generally organized into departments or divisions, based on their subject or field. They usually teach several different courses in their department, such as introduction to anthropology, folklore, museum methods, linguistics, and ethnographic methods.

Four-year university professors may teach introductory-level courses and upper-level undergraduate courses, or they may concentrate solely on graduate courses. Four-year college faculty teach introductory-level courses and upper-level undergraduate courses. Community college professors teach introductory-level courses and sometimes a few upper-level courses.

College and university faculty may lecture to several hundred students in large halls, lead small seminars, and supervise students in laboratories. They also prepare lectures, exercises, and laboratory experiments; grade exams and papers; and advise and work with students individually. They may use closed-circuit and cable television, computers, videotapes, and other teaching aids. In universities, professors also counsel, advise, teach, and supervise graduate students.

Faculty keep abreast of developments in their field by reading current literature, talking with colleagues, and participating in professional conferences. They also do research to expand knowledge in their field and then write about their findings in scholarly journals and books.

Most faculty members serve on academic or administrative committees that deal with the policies of their institution, departmental matters, academic issues, curricula, budgets, equipment purchases, and hiring. Some work with student organizations. Department heads generally have heavier administrative responsibilities.

The amount of time spent on each of these activities varies by individual circumstance and type of institution. Professors at universities generally spend a significant part of their time doing research; those in four-year colleges, somewhat less; and those in two-year colleges, relatively little. However, the teaching load usually is heavier in two-year colleges.

Possible Job Settings

Some anthropology graduates use their bachelor's degree in anthropology as a foundation to teach anthropology or the other social sciences in secondary school. They work in public school districts or for private or alternative schools.

Master's-level anthropologists may find work in community colleges. The large majority of four-year institutions hire Ph.D. holders. Academic settings in which Ph.D.-level anthropologists work include departments of anthropology and related departments such as linguistics; cultural studies; women's studies; ethnic, community, or area studies; psychology; ecology; education; and schools of medicine or public health. They also work in university research laboratories; in campus ethnic centers such as African-American centers; in campus research institutes such as demography centers, survey research institutes, or archaeology centers; and in campus museums.

Departments of anthropology at colleges and universities currently employ the largest proportion of anthropology Ph.D.s.

Sample Job Listings

The job listings will show you the range of departments and subject matter open to Ph.D. holders who desire to teach and conduct research in a university setting. Because the positions have already been filled, the names of the hiring body and contact information have been deleted.

University seeks Ph.D., Medical Anthropologist for tenure-track position, Asst Prof level for fall semester. Must specialize in Native Amer health & healing systems; be able to develop new courses; teach existing medical, cultural, & Indian Studies courses.

University seeks a Sociocultural Anthropologist with area specialization in Africa, Africa-America or Oceania. Preferred topical specialties are political, ecological, economic or transnational anthropology. This is a tenure-track position at the Asst Prof level. Completed Ph.D. is reqd. Teach six courses/yr including intro to cultural anth & an interdisciplinary intro to global studies, with opportunity also to teach in freshman interdisciplinary program. Strong preference is given to candidates with demonstrated undergrad teaching ability, & enthusiasm for teaching is essential.

University Dept of Anthropology invites applications for a tenure-track position in Cultural Anth with specialization in anthropological gerontology & applied anth, beginning fall semester. Ph.D. in anth required. Candidates must have a research focus on cultural gerontology with fieldwork experience in Asia & be qualified to teach courses such as intro to cultural anth, world cultures, peoples of Asia, cultural gerontology, & anthro fieldwork & theory.

College invites applications for a tenure-track appt in Sociocultural Anthropology with a specialty in linguistic anth, at the Asst Prof level. Candidates should have a commitment to undergrad teaching at a liberal arts college where there is an emphasis on high-quality instruction & a commitment to ongoing research. Preference will be given to applicants who connect linguistic anth with such other areas as cognitive/legal/medical anth or the anth of science, who have completed the Ph.D. & who have some teaching experience.

University Dept of Anthropology anticipates a tenure-track position in biological anth. Specialties should be in human biology with particular interests in reproductive ecology, life histories, demography, & health. Applicants should demonstrate ongoing research & publications dealing with living or nonliving human groups.

University Dept of Anthropology invites applications for a tenure-track Asst Prof position in anth with a specialization in community development & public policy. Requirements: Ph.D.; specialty in community-based development in areas such as, but not limited to, urban housing, education &/or environmental issues, economic development, nonprofits (NGO); strong methodological skills; demonstrated excellence in research, outreach, & teaching required.

University Dept of Anthropology requests applications for a tenure-track Asst Prof faculty position in Paleoanthropology. A demonstrable interdisciplinary approach to research & teaching among subdisciplines of anth, participation in an active field paleontology program, & a focus on the phylogeny & paleoecology of the Genus Homo since the early Pleistocene are required.

University Dept of Anthropology & Ethnic Studies invites applications for a full-time tenure-track Asst Prof in Museology. Particular skills should include artifact conservation, heritage resource mgmt, & a strong theoretical background. Preference will be given to candidates whose research emphasizes arid environments, who have previous teaching exp, who demonstrate an ability to obtain funding, who have experience with Native Amer/NAGPRA issues, or who have expertise in museum operations. The Ph.D. in anth must be in hand by —.

Related Occupations

Teaching requires a wide variety of skills and aptitudes, including a talent for working with people; organizational, administrative, and record-keeping abilities; research and communication skills; the ability to influence, motivate, and train others; patience; and creativity. Workers in other occupations requiring some of these aptitudes include counselors, librarians, education administrators, writers, consultants, lobbyists, policy analysts, employment interviewers, preschool workers, public relations specialists, sales representatives, social workers, trainers, and employee development specialists.

Training and Qualifications

To work in most public school systems, a bachelor's degree and teaching certification are required. Licensing or certifying of teachers in the United States is the responsibility of each individual state. Information about each state's licensing requirements can be obtained from the teacher certification office of that state. In higher education, postgraduate degrees are required.

Secondary Education

On January 8, 2002, the No Child Left Behind Act went into effect. This law is intended to improve the nation's public schools. One of the provisions of the act states "All teachers hired to teach core academic subjects must be highly qualified." This means teachers must have full certification, a bachelor's degree, and demonstrated competence in subject knowledge and teaching skills. Each state that receives federal Title II funds must devise a plan to ensure that all teachers of core subjects are highly qualified by the end of the 2005–2006 school year. Social studies is one of the core academic subjects specified by this act. For more information on this legislation see the U.S. Department of Education's website at ed.gov/nclb/landing.jhtml.

Few high schools offer anthropology courses per se. Anthropology is usually studied as part of social studies. Some schools offer a world cultures course or multicultural studies; in other schools anthropology content is integrated into history courses.

The No Child Left Behind legislation requires that secondary school teachers have a major in the subject that they teach. Therefore, anthropology majors who aspire to teach in a secondary school should have a double major in anthropology and history or some other subject taught as part of the social studies curriculum.

Student Teaching. In most colleges, student teaching occurs near the end of the education program. Student teaching programs last from eight to sixteen weeks. During that time, the student teacher works closely with an experienced teacher and his or her responsibilities gradually increase from observing and assisting to teaching a full day. The student teacher's progress is evaluated by the classroom teacher and by a representative of the university granting the teaching degree. Many educators regard the student teaching experience as the best predictor of the future teacher's performance.

Teacher Examinations. In most states, prospective teachers must pass a test before they can be certified. Tests are administered in these areas:

- **Basic skills**—proficiency in writing, reading, spelling, and math
- **Subject matter**—mastery of the material to be taught
- **Teaching skills**—understanding of the general principles of learning and education; of the social and cultural forces that influence curriculum and teaching; and of the organization and legal bases of education

Internships. In several states, a newly certified teacher must serve a year's internship in an accredited school. The beginning teacher has a full-day teaching assignment and receives regular pay and benefits. An outstanding experienced teacher, who also has a full-time teaching assignment, serves as the beginning teacher's mentor. The mentor meets regularly with the beginning teacher and provides guidance and support during the critical first year of teaching.

Continuing Certification. Almost all states require continuing education for renewal of the teacher's certificate. Some require a master's degree.

Board Certification. Teachers may become board certified by successfully completing the National Board for Professional Teaching Standards certification process. This certification is voluntary but may result in a higher salary.

Information on certification requirements and approved teacher training institutions is available from local school systems and state departments of education.

Alternative Teacher Certification. Many states offer alternative teacher certification programs for people who have college training in the subject they will teach but do not have the necessary education courses required for a regular certificate. Alternative certification programs were originally designed to ease teacher shortages in certain subjects, such as mathematics and science. The programs have expanded to attract other people into teaching, including recent college graduates and career changers.

In some programs, individuals begin teaching immediately under provisional certification. After teaching under the close supervision of experienced educators for one or two years while taking education courses outside school hours, these individuals receive regular certification if they have progressed satisfactorily. In other programs, college graduates who do not meet certification requirements take only those courses that they lack and then become certified. This may take one or two semesters of full-time study.

Aspiring teachers who need certification may also enter programs that grant a master's degree in education as well as certification. States also issue emergency certificates to individuals who do not meet all requirements for a regular certificate when schools cannot hire enough teachers.

College and University Teaching

Most college and university faculty hold one of four academic ranks: professor, associate professor, assistant professor, or instructor. A small number are lecturers.

Most faculty members are hired as instructors or assistant professors. Four-year colleges and universities generally hire doctoral degree holders for full-time, tenure-track positions, but they may hire master's degree holders or doctoral candidates for certain disciplines or for part-time and temporary jobs.

Doctoral programs usually take four to seven years of full-time study beyond the bachelor's degree. Candidates usually specialize in a subfield of a discipline—for example, cultural anthropology, medical anthropology, linguistic anthropology, or archaeology—but also take courses covering the whole discipline. Program requirements include twenty or more increasingly specialized courses and seminars; comprehensive examinations on all major areas of the field; and a dissertation, a report on original research to answer some significant question in the field. The dissertation, done under the guidance of one or more faculty advisers, usually takes several years of full-time work.

Professors of anthropology and faculty advisers suggest you go for the doctorate only if you have a passion for the field. When choosing your program, make sure it encourages close communication with faculty. Find out if faculty members regularly coauthor articles with students. Choose your dissertation committee carefully, and develop a good working relationship with your adviser. Make sure the members of your committee are compatible with you and share an interest in your work. They should be generous with their time.

You need to always think in terms of fundable research for your doctoral degree. Pick an area that is being funded by the federal government or other bodies. You shouldn't enroll in a doctoral program if you are not assured of funding.

Be careful not to let faculty members push you toward areas of study that you aren't interested in. Note, too, that often faculty members fail to discourage many students who would be far better served researching another topic; make sure you communicate well with your adviser.

Advancement

With additional preparation and certification, secondary school teachers may become administrators or supervisors, although the number of positions is limited. In some systems, highly qualified, experienced teachers can become senior or mentor teachers, with higher pay and additional responsibilities. They guide and assist less-experienced teachers while keeping most of their original teaching responsibilities.

Some college and university faculty, based on their teaching experience, research, publications, and service on campus committees and task forces, move into administrative positions, such as department chairperson, dean, and president.

Working Conditions

The following section will give you an overview of the different aspects of teaching in various settings.

Secondary Education

Secondary school teachers teach from five to seven periods in a day and may work with more than one hundred students in a day. They may also have extracurricular responsibilities, such as coaching sports or chaperoning school outings.

In most secondary schools, maintaining discipline and a positive classroom environment has become a weighty part of the teacher's role. One of the benefits to having such close contact with young students is that teachers may help shape a student's future and assist in choosing courses, colleges, and careers.

Teachers also participate in education conferences and workshops. Many enjoy several weeks' vacation during the school year and two months off in the summer. To supplement their incomes, others teach summer school or find other part-time summer work.

College and University Teaching

College faculty generally have flexible schedules. They must be present for classes, usually six to sixteen hours a week, and for faculty and committee meetings. Most establish regular office hours for student consultations, usually three to six hours per week. Otherwise, they are relatively free to decide when and where they will work and how much time to devote to course preparation, grading papers and exams, study, research, and other activities.

Professors may teach classes at night and on weekends, particularly those targeted to students who have full-time jobs or family responsibilities on weekdays. Faculty have even greater flexibility during the summer and school holidays, when they may teach, do research or fieldwork, travel, or pursue nonacademic interests. Most colleges and universities have funds to support faculty research or other professional development needs, including travel to conferences and research sites.

Part-time faculty generally spend little time on campus, since they usually don't have an office. In addition, they may teach at more than one college, requiring travel between their various places of employment.

Faculty may experience a conflict between their responsibilities to teach students and the pressure to do research. This can be a particular problem for newer faculty seeking tenure.

Career Outlook

The following will give you an idea of the employment outlook for teaching positions at both the secondary school and college/university levels.

School Systems

Social studies teachers will face stiff competition for teaching positions. However, the growing importance and popularity of social science subjects in secondary schools is strengthening the demand for teachers at this level.

Overall employment of schoolteachers is expected to increase faster than the average for all occupations through 2010, fueled by a need for special education teachers. Projected employment growth varies among individual subjects, with the largest number of openings in math and science. Job openings for all teachers are expected to increase substantially by the end of the decade as the large number of teachers now in their fifties reach retirement age.

Assuming relatively little change in average class size, employment growth for teachers depends on the rates of population growth and corresponding student enrollments. The number of fourteen- to seventeen-year-olds is expected to increase through 2006, spurring demand for secondary school teachers.

The number of teachers also is expected to increase in response to reports of improved job prospects, more teacher involvement in school policy, greater public interest in education, and higher salaries. In fact, enrollments in teacher training programs already have increased in recent years. In addition, more teachers should be available from alternative certification programs.

Some central cities and rural areas have difficulty attracting enough teachers, so job prospects should continue to be better in these areas than in suburban districts. With enrollments of minorities increasing, efforts to recruit minority teachers may intensify.

The number of teachers employed depends on state and local expenditures for education. Pressures from taxpayers to limit spending could result in fewer teachers than projected; pressures to spend more to improve the quality of education could mean more.

Higher Education

According to the American Anthropological Association, about four hundred people receive Ph.D.s in anthropology each year. In the last decade there have not been that many openings for college faculty each year. According to the *Occupational Outlook Handbook*, however, positions for college and university faculty are expected to increase faster than the average for all occupations through the year 2010. Enrollments in institutions of higher education grew in the 1980s and 1990s, as a higher proportion of eighteen- to twenty-four-year-olds, along with a growing number of part-time, female, and older students, attended college. Enrollments are expected to continue to grow through the year 2010 as the baby-boom "echo" generation (children of the baby boomers) reaches college age.

Positions will also open as faculty members retire; the large number of faculty who entered the profession during the 1960s are reaching retirement age. Most faculty members likely to retire are full-time tenured professors. However, some institutions are expected to cut costs either by leaving some of these positions vacant or by hiring part-time or temporary faculty members as replacements. Job applicants should be prepared to face competition for jobs as Ph.D. graduates vie for fewer full-time tenure-track openings.

The financial difficulties faced by colleges and universities are likely to continue. Many states have reduced funding for higher education. As a result, the trend of hiring adjunct or part-time faculty to save money on salary and benefits is also likely to continue.

Employment of college faculty is also related to the nonacademic job market through an echo effect. Excellent job prospects in a field—for example, computer science from the late 1970s to the mid-1980s—cause more students to enroll in that program, increasing faculty needs. On the other hand, poor job prospects in a field, such as history in recent years, discourage students and reduce demand for faculty.

Earnings

Salary expectations will depend on whether you are teaching in a secondary school or in an institution of higher education.

School Systems

According to the American Federation of Teachers, beginning teachers with a bachelor's degree earned an average of $30,719 in 2001–2002. The average salary of all public school teachers in 2001–2002 was $44,367. California had the highest average salary at $54,000; South Dakota the lowest at $31,000. More than half of all public school teachers belong to a union, usually affiliated with either the American Federation of Teachers or the National Education Association, which may result in higher teacher salaries. Salaries in private schools tend to be lower than those in public schools.

In some schools, teachers receive extra pay for coaching sports or for working with students in extracurricular activities. Some teachers earn extra income during the summer working in the school system or in other jobs.

Higher Education

Earnings in colleges and universities vary according to faculty rank and the type of institution and, in some cases, by field. Economics professors, for example, often have higher salaries than anthropology professors because economists have more opportunities for employment in business, finance, and government. Faculty in four-year institutions earn higher salaries, on average, than those in two-year schools, and faculty in doctoral-granting universities earn more than those in colleges that only offer bachelor's degrees. According to a 2002–2003 survey by the American Association of University Professors, salaries for full-time faculty on nine-month contracts averaged $65,000. By rank, the average for professors was $86,000; associate professors, $61,700; assistant professors, $51,500; lecturers, $43,900; and instructors, $37,700.

Many faculty members have added earnings, both during the academic year and the summer, from teaching additional courses, conducting research, consulting, writing for publication, or other employment.

Most college and university faculty enjoy some unique benefits, including access to campus facilities, tuition waivers for dependents, travel allowances, and paid sabbatical leaves. Part-time faculty have fewer benefits than full-time faculty; they usually do not receive health insurance, retirement benefits, or sabbatical leave.

Some college and university professors are members of unions, such as the American Association of University Professors or the American Federation of Teachers.

Close-Ups

These firsthand accounts from anthropologists show how they are using their degrees and skills in a variety of interesting educational settings.

James Dow—Professor

James Dow is a professor at Oakland University. Among the courses he teaches are Introduction to Cultural Anthropology, Cultures of Mexico and Central America, Ethnographic Methods, Indians of South America, Medical Anthropology, and Mesoamerican Archaeology. He earned his B.S. in mathematics at Massachusetts Institute of Technology in 1957 and his Ph.D. in cultural anthropology at Brandeis University in 1973.

Getting Started. "A bachelor's in anthropology is not necessary for pursuing study at the doctorate level. I was interested in doing research in a science that is more humanistic than applied mathematics."

The Realities of the Job. "A university job in anthropology is very much like an academic job in any other field. The nature of the job depends much more on the university for which you work than on the discipline in which you teach and do research.

"Universities also differ among themselves in the degree to which they emphasize research versus writing. The few large, old universities emphasize scholarship as expressed in writing more than anything else. In anthropology this usually takes the form of producing books. At the more numerous younger universities that do not have a hoary reputation to maintain, the pressure to publish will be much less.

"The most coveted jobs at universities are the ones that lead to tenure. Tenure guarantees that you will not be fired; however, you have to prove the quality of your teaching and scholarship before being granted tenure. This usually takes five or more years. If you do not receive tenure, you generally have to leave the university.

"Before getting tenure, faculty members usually have to prove that they can produce scholarship of a quality that gets their work published in good journals. Quality teaching is also important.

"Before and after tenure, a university faculty person works very hard. They may concentrate on doing new research, setting up academic programs, supervising student research, or teaching. There is a great opportunity to know students and help them mature personally and intellectually. Many faculty find great rewards in this.

"I usually spend ten or twelve hours a day doing something related to my job. I work as much as I can without jeopardizing my family life or friendships. This means that I usually work at something in the evening or on the weekends. It is often hard to define the boundary between work and leisure.

"I may be watching television and come across a well-put-together documentary. I may be reading a news magazine and find some research that is relevant to my interests. Many of my hobbies interrelate with my work. A new computer 'toy' often helps me in my job. My enjoyment of creative photography has been very helpful. I found that my ham radio was also useful when doing fieldwork.

"The least pleasant part of my work is the bureaucratic requirements of my job. These do not bother everybody, and many faculty enjoy participating in the bureaucratic structure of the university. Fortunately, I do not work for a university in which management treats the faculty like employees. It is important to work for a university in which academic values, which include positive experiences for students, are put first.

"I don't like to give exams and hand out grades. I would like all my students to be fascinated by cultural anthropology and do the best they can, but, alas, they have varied goals and interests. Human nature places limits on the freedom that one can give to students, and therefore the structure of teaching can be a burden at times.

"The most important thing to me is the freedom to investigate and write about things that I think are significant to me and the rest of the human race. I can burrow under social, political, and economic systems to see how they work."

Salaries. "One starting out can expect to earn around $35,000 per year. Salaries can go up to $70,000 and into six figures at the wealthiest and most prestigious universities. The skills held by most faculty can bring in twice as much in the business world if used competitively."

Advice from James Dow. "Check to see what the unemployment level is for the degree you are pursuing. Cultural anthropology can have a rather high level of Ph.D. unemployment.

"Be honest in examining your motives. Ask yourself if you are willing to put up with long years of graduate education, long years of fieldwork, and then long years of job hunting. You will probably have to move to find a job. Cultural anthropologists are expected to enjoy living in foreign countries in rural underdeveloped areas."

Richard Meindl—Professor and Department Chairperson

Richard Meindl has been with the Department of Anthropology at Kent State University since 1998. He earned his B.A. in mathematics and his M.A. in anthropology at Kent State in 1969 and 1973, respectively, and his Ph.D. in physical anthropology from the University of Massachusetts in 1979.

Getting Started. "As a senior in an undergraduate program in mathematics, I took my first anthropology course. My particular career was a direct result of course electives I took as an undergraduate. I found archaeology, human evolution, paleoanthropology, and primate anatomy to be very exciting.

"I elected to go on a summer field school in archaeology in 1970. But I have to admit that it was by pure chance that I wound up in this field.

"Remarkably, my job at Kent is the first and only professional position that I have held since graduate school. This sort of career trajectory is unusual."

The Realities of the Job. "This job is first-rate! Imagine working on a variety of research projects both alone and with colleagues. I also enjoy management—being the chairperson of the department.

"My duties include teaching and student advising at all levels: undergraduate, master's, and doctoral programs. I teach both human evolution and statistics, each providing a nice change of pace from the other.

"I research questions about human evolution and biological demography. I publish regularly in both of these areas.

"The bulk of my day is devoted to administrative things. My department comprises seven full-time faculty and four part-time faculty. Since we are an unusually small department, the administrative duties are not oppressive.

"All of my faculty do a very good job in terms of both scholarship and teaching. We now have a fully renovated building: new classrooms, offices, and laboratories. Therefore, morale is quite high.

"My first love in anthropology was teaching and research. Despite my administrative duties, these remain my primary interests. What is most rewarding about biological anthropology is the variety. This applies to both research and the classroom. In a typical human evolution course, I cover molecular genetics, then evolutionary theory, then modern human variation, then nonhuman primate behavior and evolution, and finish up with human paleontology. By the time a student (or an instructor) becomes bored with one of those topics, we're on to the next one.

"Research is similar. I collaborate with colleagues in skeletal biology, historic demography, and human paleontology."

Salaries. "With the chairperson's additional stipend, I earn over $70K. New faculty members hired now (fresh out of graduate school with a doctorate in hand) would earn perhaps $40K the first year."

Advice from Richard Meindl. "The salaries I mentioned are not large, especially for professionals who spend anywhere from four to eight years earning a Ph.D. Therefore, you had better love (1) the academic life and (2) your chosen field of specialization. There are a lot of ways to earn a lot more money outside of life at the university."

Strategies for Finding the Jobs

The following resources can help you in your job search.

College Career Placement Centers

Check for job postings at your college career office. Career offices routinely receive mailings of job openings. You can also leave your résumé on file there. Prospective employers regularly contact college career offices for likely candidates.

Classified Ads

Seek out the classified ads in all newspapers in your area or in the geographic location in which you'd prefer to work. A trip to the library will reveal periodicals you might not have been aware of. Many newspapers can be found online.

The Internet

The Internet is an incredible source for job hunting. You will discover a wealth of information online—professional associations with job banks and job placement services; educational institutions listing their job openings; professional publications, such as newsletters and journals, with job listings; and a wide variety of potential employers and job search services—most of which are available to you at no charge.

For jobs in higher education, check out such specialized organizations as the American Association of Physical Anthropologists (physanth.org) and the Biological Anthropology Web (bioanth.org/careers).

Internships and Volunteering

Anthropology educators will find internships and volunteering stints to be important keys to finding work in many different settings. You can read more about internship possibilities in the other chapters in this book.

The *Chronicle of Higher Education*

The *Chronicle of Higher Education* is the old standby for people seeking positions within two- and four-year colleges and universities. It is a weekly publication available by subscription, in libraries or your college placement office, and online at chronicle.com.

Placement Agencies

Placement agencies can provide a valuable source for finding employment, particularly for private schools, both at home and abroad. Some charge both the employer and the prospective employee a fee; others charge just one or the other.

Resources

American Anthropological Association
2200 Wilson Blvd., Suite 600
Arlington, VA 22201
aaanet.org

American Association for Higher Education
One Dupont Cir. NW, Suite 360
Washington, DC 20036
aahe.org

American Association of University Professors
1012 Fourteenth St. NW, Suite 500
Washington, DC 20005
aaup.org

American Federation of Teachers
555 New Jersey Ave. NW
Washington, DC 20001
aft.org

Association of American Colleges and Universities
1818 R St. NW
Washington, DC 20009
aacu-edu.org

The *Chronicle of Higher Education*
1255 23rd St. NW, Suite 700
Washington, DC 20037
chronicle.com

Council for American Private Education
13017 Wisteria Dr., #457
Germantown, MD 20874
capenet.org

National Association of Independent Schools
1620 L St. NW, Suite 1100
Washington, DC 20036
nais.org

National Board for Professional Teaching Standards
1525 Wilson Blvd., Suite 500
Arlington, VA 22209
nbpts.org

National Council for Accreditation of Teacher Education
2010 Massachusetts Ave. NW, Suite 500
Washington, DC 20036
ncate.org

National Council for the Social Studies
8555 Sixteenth St., Suite 500
Silver Spring, MD 20910
ncss.org

National Education Association
1201 Sixteenth St. NW
Washington, DC 20036
nea.org

8

Path 3: Archaeology

Archaeology is currently the most popular subfield of anthropology. Archaeologists study the artifacts of past cultures to learn about their history, customs, and living habits. Archaeologists survey and excavate archaeological sites, recording and cataloging their finds. By careful analysis, they reconstruct earlier cultures and determine their influence on the present.

Archaeologists have long been interested in the classical societies of Greece, Rome, and Egypt, but they have also extended their studies backward some three million years to the bones and stone tools of our predecessors, and forward to the lifestyles and communities of nineteenth-century America. However, archaeologists don't limit their studies to just these regions and time periods; virtually every area of the world comes under archaeological scrutiny.

Archaeological sites are the physical remains of past civilizations. They can include building debris and the items found inside, as well as the trash heaps outside. Usually these sites have been buried by later human activity or by natural processes.

Excavation of archaeological sites is a painstaking process conducted by professionals using modern techniques. Because these sites are so fragile, the very nature of excavating destroys some information. With this in mind, archaeologists are careful to dig only as much as they need to answer important questions.

Definition of the Career Path

The science of archaeology serves to satisfy our curiosity about the past. The methods archaeologists use are not unlike those of a Sherlock Holmes seeking clues. More and more people are becoming fascinated with the field, interested in learning more about the past through archaeology and in participating in archaeological investigations.

Archaeology is a subfield of anthropology, but it also has its own subfields.

American archaeology is the study of archaeological sites in the New World (North, Meso-, Central, and South America).

Archaeobotany is the study of plant remains from archaeological sites.

Archaeometry is the field in which analytical techniques and scientific methods from such fields as chemistry, geology, geophysics, biology, and engineering are applied to a variety of archaeological problems. It includes any quantitative analytical method used to understand artifacts, including dating methods and trace element studies.

Classical archaeology is the study of classical Greece and the Roman Empire, but it is sometimes broadened to include Egypt, the Near East, and other Old World civilizations, such as India and China.

Cultural resource management (CRM) is also known as contract archaeology. It refers to the excavation and study of sites prior to their destruction by development projects or to facilitate their preservation on state or federal land. In contract archaeology, funding is provided to study particular sites to meet legal or regulatory requirements. This work is often contracted out to private companies by government agencies. CRM includes the study of sites that will be adversely affected by construction or development. In some cases, if an important site is discovered, the development can be relocated, such as by rerouting a road. In other cases, artifacts are recovered from the site before it is destroyed, by flooding from a dam, for example.

Ethnoarchaeology is the study of contemporary societies to learn how archaeological sites are formed and how material objects are obtained, made, used, and discarded.

Experimental archaeology includes a variety of kinds of studies that research how something was done in the past, such as making a stone tool or building a pyramid. It also includes efforts to identify wear patterns on artifacts as a result of their use, for example, experimental butchering studies to see how use modifies the edge of a stone tool or the butchered bone.

Historical archaeology is concerned with the excavation and analysis of sites that were occupied during historic times; in other words, since the development of written records. The term is often used to refer to sites that had contact with or were colonized by European countries. Historical archaeology has the advantage of access to historical documents to facilitate interpretation.

Landscape archaeology is a fairly new discipline whose purpose is to recover enough evidence to re-create a garden that existed on a site in a given historical period. Landscape archaeology uses traditional archaeological technique to recover fence lines, planting beds, and other evidence.

Maritime archaeology is the study of the material remains of people and their activities at sea. Also see the definitions of nautical archaeology and underwater archaeology.

Medieval archaeology is the study of sites dating to the medieval period in Europe.

Nautical archaeology is the study of shipwreck sites, either on land or underwater. Also see the definitions of maritime archaeology and underwater archaeology.

Paleobotany is the analysis and interpretation of archaeobotanical remains to explain the interaction between humans and plants.

Paleoethnobotany is the study of past cultures by an examination of the interactions between the human population and the plant world.

Underwater archaeology is the study and excavation of submerged sites. Usually these are shipwrecks, but underwater archaeology includes the study of submerged habitation sites as well. Also see the definitions of nautical archaeology and maritime archaeology.

Zooarchaeology is the study of animal remains from archaeological sites, including the analysis of hunting and butchering activities and the disposition of animal carcasses.

Archaeologists conducting fieldwork often work with several other professionals in a team effort. They are assisted by geologists, ethnologists, educators, anthropologists, ecologists, and aerial photographers.

In the field, archaeologists use a variety of tools during an excavation. These include picks, shovels, trowels, wheelbarrows, sifting boxes, pressure sprayers, and brushes. Archaeologists also make drawings and sketches on-site as well as take notes and photographs.

Possible Employers

Although most people imagine archaeologists mainly performing outdoor fieldwork, archaeologists find employment in a variety of work settings with a variety of job titles, such as educator, researcher, administrator, and consultant.

The following list features regular employers of archaeologists:

County and city government restoration programs
Cultural resource management firms
Engineering firms
Environmental agencies
Historic architecture firms
Museums
Private and public foundations
Private archaeological consulting firms
State departments of conservation
State departments of natural resources
State departments of transportation
State historic preservation offices
State parks and recreation departments
Universities and colleges
Urban and city planning offices
U.S. Army Corps of Engineers
U.S. Bureau of Land Management
U.S. Bureau of Reclamation
U.S. Forest Service
U.S. National Park Service

Within colleges and universities, archaeologists are found in departments of anthropology, archaeology, art history, architecture, classics, history, and theology. The positions may involve undergraduate and graduate teaching, fieldwork, laboratory research, conservation, and curating of collections.

Possible Job Settings

In the academic field, most faculty positions are nine-month appointments. During the summer, many academic archaeologists conduct field research funded by grants or contracts, teach summer field schools, or work as private consultants. Research money may come from the archaeologist's university, from federal agencies such as the National Science Foundation and the National Endowment for the Humanities, or from private foundations such as the National Geographic Society and Earthwatch.

A Ph.D. is required for faculty positions at colleges and universities. A master's is required for community college positions. Chapter 7 gives far more information about working within a university setting.

Within museums, archaeologists work as curators, conservators, exhibit designers, and public educators. Museums may be independently run or connected with a university. Museum positions generally require a graduate degree. More information about museum work is found in Chapter 9.

Within the public sector—city, state, and federal government agencies—archaeologists work on a variety of projects in a variety of departments. The U.S. Forest Service, National Park Service, Bureau of Land Management, and the U.S. Army Corps of Engineers currently employ about eight hundred archaeologists.

Each of the fifty states has a state historic preservation office with one or more archaeologists on staff. State parks departments, highway departments, and water resource departments also employ archaeologists.

Some cities also employ archaeologists to comply with local ordinances protecting archaeological sites. Construction projects, such as the building of new highways, often require surveys to locate prehistoric or historic sites. Then excavation must be conducted before construction can begin.

Within the private sector, archaeologists work for firms that conduct the CRM investigations required by law. They conduct archaeological surveys to locate prehistoric and historic sites. They also excavate significant sites prior to their destruction by construction activities.

Archaeologists may work in the field, in laboratories analyzing the results of their investigations, or in an office, writing reports on those investigations and findings, and preparing proposals for grants or other research monies to conduct additional work.

Private-sector archaeologists find employment within private laboratories or with engineering and environmental firms. They also work for companies that specialize in archaeological investigations, and they work as private consultants.

These private (as well as government) organizations also employ field archaeologists or technicians as temporary staff to assist with field investigations. Field positions usually require a bachelor's degree and experience in an archaeological field school.

The following table outlines the four major sectors in which archaeologists work, their duties, and their working conditions.

There are now more archaeologists working in CRM or contract archaeology than in colleges and universities teaching archaeology. Increasing numbers of federal grants and contracts have been made available for archaeological fieldwork and research. Much of this work is being conducted in the western and southwestern states, such as Colorado, Arizona, and New Mexico. In northwestern New Mexico in particular, there is a significant industry developing resources such as gas and oil. Because much of the land

Setting	Duties	Working Conditions
Universities and colleges, private institutions	Teaching, fieldwork, research, directing student research and fieldwork	Classroom, labs, office space
Museums	Fieldwork, research, classifying, preserving, displaying	Display and research areas, office space, labs
Public sector (local, state, and federal government agencies)	Excavating, surveying, analyzing, preserving and recording remains	On site, labs, research facilities
Private sector (construction companies, architectural firms)	Excavating, surveying, preserving and recording remains	On site, labs, research facilities

there is owned by the Bureau of Land Management, oil exploration companies have to hire professional archaeologists to study the site before gas lines can be put in or wells drilled.

In addition, the building of a reservoir on the Dolores River in Colorado uncovered hundreds of archaeological sites, necessitating a great deal of archaeological work. The project, which is the largest on the continent, has a very attractive budget and brought many archaeologists to that area.

Training and Qualifications

Preparing for a career in archaeology involves both academic training and practical experience.

Most jobs with career-advancement potential require a master's degree, although some positions are available for those with a bachelor's degree with a major in anthropology or archaeology and field experience, which is usually obtained by spending a summer in an archaeological field school or participating as a volunteer. (See "Participating in Archaeology" later in this chapter.)

While a bachelor's degree and experience is sufficient to work on an archaeological field crew, it is not usually enough to allow the worker to move into a supervisory role. Supervisory positions with more responsibility require either a master's or a doctorate. Upon the completion of a Ph.D., some archaeologists do postdoctoral work.

In deciding where to study archaeology, many factors should be taken into account, such as departmental specialties, required and related course offerings, the size of the program, and the cost. Interests and career objectives should be weighed against the offerings of the university.

In most universities, the archaeology program either is housed in a department of its own or is within the anthropology department. A useful resource for finding universities that give degrees in archaeology is the "AAA Guide" published by the American Anthropological Association. The address is listed at the end of this chapter.

David Carlson, associate professor of anthropology at Texas A&M University, offers this advice on preparing for a career in archaeology:

"Education and training requirements are different for different kinds of archaeology. In the United States, anthropology departments include archaeology as one of four subdisciplines. During the late nineteenth and early twentieth centuries, anthropology programs in the United States were established to study American Indian societies, languages, and ruins. As a result, there are few separate archaeology departments; interdisciplinary programs that combine archaeology with various other fields of study are more common. Students who wish to study ancient or classical civilizations (including the Near East, Egypt, early civilizations of the Mediterranean, classical Greece and Rome, and the early civilizations of India, China, and Southeast Asia) are more likely to pursue their studies in interdisciplinary programs that include courses in art, architecture, classics, history, ancient and modern languages, and theology. Students who wish to study the historical periods (roughly from the fall of Rome to the present) combine history (including archival and oral history research) with courses in historical and vernacular architecture, material culture and folklore, and archaeology.

"At the undergraduate level, there is little specialization. A major in anthropology requires courses in all of the subdisciplines. For students interested in ancient and classical civilizations, the particular undergraduate major is not important, but it is advantageous to begin learning several ancient and modern languages (e.g., Greek, Latin, German, French). Historical archaeologists usually major in anthropology or history. An undergraduate degree (B.A./B.S.) is sufficient to work as a field archaeologist in the United States and to perform basic laboratory studies. Experience through participation in an archaeological field school or as a volunteer is often required. Summer archaeological field schools provide the best way to learn how to properly excavate and record archaeological sites and to find out if archaeology is really for you.

"Job opportunities outside the United States are very limited, but volunteers with field experience should be welcome almost anywhere. Most foreign governments will issue excavation permits only to archaeologists with a Ph.D. degree.

"There are two levels of graduate training in archaeology. The first is an M.A. or M.S. degree, which takes about one to two years of course work beyond the B.A./B.S. degree and a written thesis that presents the results of original research by the student. Some programs offer a nonthesis M.A. degree. Unless you are planning to work immediately on a Ph.D. degree, the preparation of a thesis is an important part of the educational process. An M.A./M.S. would be enough to direct field crews and is sufficient for many government positions in archaeology. It is also sufficient to work in the private sector, to teach in a community college, and to work for some museums.

"An M.A./M.S. with a thesis and a year of field and laboratory experience is the minimum for certification by the Register of Professional Archaeologists.

"The second graduate degree is the Ph.D., which is required to teach in a college or university or hold a museum curatorship. The Ph.D. degree requires two to three years of courses beyond the M.A. and the successful preparation and oral defense of a dissertation containing original research in your chosen specialization within the field of archaeology. As mentioned, some graduate programs offer streamlined tracks for students with a B.A. degree so that they work directly toward a Ph.D., while others require an M.A. degree first."

Sample Program List

In addition to the American Anthropological Association's yearly department guide, the "Guide to Higher Education in Historical and Underwater Archaeology" is updated annually on the website of the Society for Historical Archaeology at sha.org/futures/higher.htm.

The following is a partial list of institutions offering graduate programs in historical and underwater archaeology:

Boston University
Brown University
College of William and Mary

Columbia University
East Carolina University
Louisiana State University
Michigan State University
Sonoma State University
State University of New York–Binghamton
Syracuse University
Texas A&M University
University of Arizona
University of California–Berkeley
University of Florida
University of Georgia
University of Maine–Orono
University of Maryland–College Park
University of Pennsylvania
University of South Carolina
Washington University

Skills

The following skills are necessary for potential archaeologists:

- Above-average academic ability
- Avid interest in science and history
- Physical strength and stamina
- Leadership qualities
- Ability to think logically and analytically
- Ability to work both independently and as part of a team
- Strong professional ethics
- Adaptability

Participating in Archaeology

Many opportunities exist to participate in archaeology through field schools or taking part in volunteer archaeology programs. These are open to students in any major as well as to people who don't want a full-time archaeological career but would still like to experience archaeological work.

If you are willing to invest your time and, in some cases, your money, you can easily find professionally supervised archaeological investigations taking on volunteers. *Archaeology* magazine provides a list of such investigations. Some other avenues to find field schools or volunteer opportunities are:

1. Check with your state archaeological or historical society. They may have annual field schools.

2. Contact Passport in Time Clearinghouse, a program in which volunteers work with archaeologists in the National Forest Service on a variety of projects. Opportunities are listed on their website at passportintime.com. They also publish a free newsletter, "PIT Traveler" twice a year, which can be ordered from the Clearinghouse at P.O. Box 31315, Tucson, AZ 85751-1315 or by calling 800-281-9176.

3. The Archaeological Institute of America publishes an annual "Archaeological Fieldwork Opportunities Bulletin" or AFOB. It is available online at archaeological.org/webinfo.php?page=10015. It can be ordered in book form from Oxbow/David Brown Books at oxbowbooks.com or by calling 800-791-9354.

4. Search the Internet. A number of projects seeking students and volunteers can be found on the Archaeological Fieldwork Server at archaeologyfieldwork.com.

5. Several organizations place volunteers and students into archaeological field projects directed by professional archaeologists:

Anasazi Heritage Center
Bureau of Land Management
27501 Hwy 184
Dolores, CO 81323
co.blm.gov/ahc/index.htm

Center for American Archaeology
P.O. Box 366
Kampsville, IL 62053
caa-archeology.org

Crow Canyon Archaeological Center
23390 Road K
Cortez, CO 81321
crowcanyon.org

Earthwatch International
P.O. Box 75
Maynard, MA 01754
earthwatch.org

Four Corners School of Outdoor Education
P.O. Box 1029
Monticello, UT 84535
fourcornersschool.org

University Research Expeditions Program
1333 Research Park Dr.
University of California
Davis, CA 95616
extension.ucdavis.edu/urep

Career Outlook

A recent survey of anthropology department chairs reveals that archaeology will grow faster than the other subfields. However, the employment picture changes year by year. Dr. James Dow, professor in the Department of Anthropology at Oakland University, reports: "A decade ago, many jobs were being created by legal requirements for environmental impact assessments. This resulted in lots of employment for people trained in archaeology and environmental studies. Many other lines of employment have opened up since then, and cultural resource management accounts for a smaller proportion of employment."

Even so, the laws means to protect cultural heritage continue to generate CRM activity, providing summer and academic-year employment. Many jobs are available for undergraduates, but they may be short-term, field-season positions.

Earnings

According to a survey by the National Association of Colleges and Employers, people with a bachelor's degree in a social science field received starting offers averaging about $25,000 a year.

In the federal government, social scientists with a bachelor's degree and no experience can start at $27,000 a year, depending on their college records. Those with a master's degree start at $36,000, and those having a doctorate begin at $48,000. Top positions with the federal government offer salaries in excess of $60,000. Beginning salaries were slightly higher in selected areas of the country where the prevailing local pay level was higher.

Starting salaries for positions with state and local agencies range from $25,000 to about $30,000 for master's degree holders.

College and university teaching and research positions range from $37,000 to $75,000 and more, and a doctorate is usually required.

Salaries in the private sector are more difficult to estimate but are usually about 30 percent higher than those in colleges and universities.

Close-Ups

The following firsthand accounts from archaeologists show how they are using their degrees and skills in a variety of interesting settings.

Kristin Kuckelman—Senior Research Archaeologist

Crow Canyon Archaeological Center is a nonprofit research and educational institution funded by tuition fees, donations, and federal grants. The center has an eighty-acre campus in southwestern Colorado, near Mesa Verde National Park, with a staff of about fifty archaeologists, educators, and support personnel. In addition to their own research, staff members instruct adults and children who want to learn about archaeology. From junior high age on up, participants are taken into the field and taught excavation, recording, and documentation techniques. They also work in the lab a few days a week learning analysis techniques and methods for cleaning artifacts.

Children too young to work in the field can still participate in a simulated dig in a lab that the center has set up for that purpose. There they can learn excavating techniques as they sift through large, shallow sandboxes where artifacts and walls and other features are buried, just as they would be in the field.

Participants come from all over the United States on educational vacations and stay for a three- to five-day program. The center also works with about a dozen graduate students of archaeology each year, providing rewarding internships.

In Montezuma County, where Crow Canyon is located, there are more than ten thousand archaeological sites. Crow Canyon professionals are currently working at two nearby sites—Sand Canyon Pueblo and Castle Rock

Pueblo, both on Bureau of Land Management land. The sites were once Anasazi Indian villages. The Anasazi are the ancestors of present-day Pueblo Indians and were in this area of Colorado from the sixth century until about the year 1300. The Crow Canyon team's research is focusing on when exactly the Anasazi left and why. They are also investigating the political and social systems of the Anasazi.

Getting Started. Kristin Kuckelman is senior research archaeologist at Crow Canyon Archaeological Center. Her interest in the field began when she was a child. Kristin's father was in the U.S. Air Force, and she traveled with her parents around the world. They were interested in different cultures and passed that interest on to their daughter. When it came time to go to college, Kristin was naturally drawn to anthropology. She graduated in 1975 with a B.A. in anthropology and psychology from Colorado Women's College and earned her master's degree in anthropology with a concentration in archaeology from the University of Texas in 1977.

The Realities of the Job. "I love the variety of it. I enjoy working outdoors; I enjoy writing. And with any kind of research, there's the excitement of discovery. You're trying to solve problems, you're trying to find things out, you're trying to learn something new. Basically, every time you go into the field, you hope you're going to learn something about a culture that no one knew before.

"The sites in this particular area are very easy to discern. They have many hundreds of masonry rooms with, even after centuries, telltale piles of rubble and thousands of artifacts scattered about the ground. Just walking around, you can see the tops of the walls and the depressions in the ground indicating the subterranean chambers.

"Because of the subterranean chambers, we sometimes have to dig down to two and a half to three meters to find the actual floor of the structure. The surface rooms are shallower, but we can still have from a meter to a meter and a half filled in.

"We've found lithic artifacts, which are artifacts made out of stone, such as spear and arrow points and sandstone tools for grinding grain. We've also found tens of thousands of pottery fragments—very rarely do we find a piece that is still intact. And very rarely do we engage in refitting, trying to piece the shards together. With so many pieces scattered over the ground, it would take many years; be very expensive; and certainly drive someone crazy!

"Beginning with the first week in May, which is the start of our field season, my partner and I head out to the site, set up equipment, and make sure we have the areas to be excavated all laid out and prepared. We take care of all our paperwork and any mapping we have to do so we're ready for participants to begin digging. During the digging season, we take participants out two or three days a week, but the first full day is spent on campus. Our educators give them a full orientation to archaeology in general. Out in the field, we conduct a site tour to give them a background on what it is we're going to be digging, why we're digging, and what we're trying to learn. We then give them tools and individual instruction, and place them, either individually or in pairs, at the particular places we want to have excavated.

"Basically, we move dirt and put it in a bucket and then take it to a screening station. The dirt gets sifted through a quarter inch mesh screen to make sure we're not losing any artifacts. Everybody has his or her own bag to keep artifacts from each excavation area separate.

"Near the end of the season, we have quite a bit of documentation and mapping to do, and we wash and analyze the artifacts. When we're finished with them, most of the artifacts are put in storage, though a few are rotated as exhibits at the Anasazi Heritage Center, a federally run curatorial facility.

"Then we have to fill the areas we've dug back in with all the screened dirt and rocks that we originally dug out. The idea is if you were to walk across the site a year later, you'd never know there had been an excavation there. For safety reasons, we can't leave gaping holes in the land, and in terms of conservation, to leave a pit open to the elements would damage the site. Before we close it back up, we line the pit with landscaping fabric to protect it, and to provide a clue in case future archaeologists are digging there but do not have access to our notes and maps. The lining would show them that the site had already been excavated. There are so many sites, to keep a site open and developed for public exhibit, as has been done at Mesa Verde, would be extremely expensive. Constant maintenance would have to be performed, or everything would eventually deteriorate.

"During the winter, we write up in report form everything we learned the previous summer. We also write articles for professional journals and present papers at archaeological conferences across the country."

Tiffanie Bourassa—Archeological Technician
Tiffanie Bourassa has been an archeological technician and an administrative clerk (the General Services classifications) with the Southeast Archeological Center (SEAC) in Tallahassee, Florida, run by the National Park Service.

She graduated in the spring of 1999 from Florida State University with a B.S. in biology with an emphasis in marine biology, a B.S. in chemical science, and a minor in anthropology.

Getting Started. "While I was a student at Florida State University, I decided to take one 'fun' class a semester. I started with underwater archaeology, and I was hooked. During one of the classes, we had a guest speaker from the National Park Service's Southeast Archeological Center. At the end of his speech, he mentioned that he was desperate for volunteers to help analyze some prehistoric seashells from a site on St. John in the Virgin Islands. After class, I spoke with him and told him that I was not an anthropology student but that I was interested. He let me start working the next day. After volunteering for a year, I was offered a student appointment position, and I'm still here!

"Once I began volunteering at SEAC, the archaeologists as well as the master's students working there helped train me. I continued to take anthropology courses to get a better understanding of the materials I was working with. I soon found that among all of the fascinating areas in anthropology, I was drawn to zooarchaeology in particular. Prehistoric sites are exciting because a lot can be told from the animal remains left behind in old trash heaps (what they were eating, what the local ecological zones were like, etc.)."

The Realities of the Job. "Over the years, I have covered just about every aspect of the archaeological process at SEAC. I have excavated sites in the field, processed artifacts (i.e., washing, preserving, bagging, labeling), analyzed artifacts, written reports, entered data into a database, processed materials for curating, and planned and organized a large-scale dig. I've also been involved with purchasing and budget planning and helped in the administrative area of the center as well.

"Each archaeologist has a specialty, and students help them in their work. One archaeologist I worked for monitors archaeology contracts on military bases. This led to diversity in my daily tasks. Some days, I entered lithic point measurements from North America into the computer, while other days, I played diplomat with angry army officials. We spent the summer excavating several sites in the U.S. Virgin Islands on a remote island. We spent the next year washing, sorting, labeling, and analyzing the artifacts recovered from the sites. The artifacts recovered do not have any monetary value, but the knowledge gained from a successful archaeological dig is priceless.

"Other tasks I perform on a regular basis are scanning photographic images from the archaeological field excavations, many mindless hours at the photocopy machine, creating and cleaning up databases, editing and formatting archaeological reports, helping people figure out what is wrong with their computer, purchasing equipment for the center, and begging for more funding. I also pick up roadkill and macerate the carcasses to add to our comparative specimen collection.

"Most of my time is spent at the office parked in front of a computer. The digging is the easy part. What you do with the artifacts and the information obtained can take a very long time.

"I enjoy the challenges I face from day to day. The upside is that I get great experience with many aspects of archaeology, I have the opportunity to coauthor papers and I am able to work with some of the top archaeologists in the country.

"The downside is the long hours involved from the beginning to the end of an archaeological project, the long days in the field away from your family, and the difficulty in finding a partner who is willing to put up with your crazy hours and periods away from home. Usually archaeologists marry archaeologists because no one else understands them (I was lucky to find a workaholic scientist who is constantly traveling)."

Earnings. "The job of 'archeological technician' is a nonpermanent position in the federal government, reserved for students in a college program. Work schedules fluctuate between twenty and forty hours per week, depending on the course load of the student. The position has a GS-5 step 1 rating. The current salary for a GS-5-1 is $23,794. After several years at the center, I was given a permanent position as an administrative clerk."

Advice from Tiffanie Bourassa. "Read everything you can get your hands on. Not only should you read books on your area of interest, but read outside of it as well. Read about the people and cultures of different time periods and geographical locations. Read historical accounts; read historical fiction. Reading also helps develop your writing skills. All those great sites and discoveries must be written up eventually.

"Volunteer. Working for free helped me land my current job. Even if there is not an archaeological center in your area, there are always opportunities. Every state has a state archaeologist who can be contacted, and you can find archaeological societies in almost every state. Field programs are always looking for volunteers, and private archaeological companies might need laborers as well. All of these experiences help make you look inviting to future employers. I have learned more in my years at SEAC than I could have ever learned in college.

"Go to conferences and network. This is where you make the best connections. You do not have to be an archaeologist to attend conferences. The fact that you are showing up demonstrates your interest—but do not let it stop there. Sell yourself. Introduce yourself to speakers you were motivated by, and let them know your interests and why they have inspired you."

Strategies for Finding the Jobs

In addition to the job-hunting strategies at the end of Chapter 5, consider fieldwork volunteering or internship experience. Being in the right place at the right time can and does happen.

Take advantage of the resources provided to you at the end of this chapter. Most of the professional associations provide job search services or list openings in newsletters and other bulletins. The Society for American Archaeology, for example, lists many available positions on its website at saa.org/careers/job-listing.html.

Here are just a few examples of the types of jobs advertised on this website. Because the positions have already been filled, the names of the hiring body and contact information have been deleted.

A university department of anthropology seeks a postdoctoral researcher in southwestern archaeology for a one-year position. The successful applicant will work with faculty and students in the development of a Web-based portal for southwestern anthropology and teach one class during the academic year that combines any aspect of archaeology and information technology. A skill in geographic information systems, relational database design, or visualization is required.

A project manager to assist in the development of a cultural resource program for a company. Conduct cultural resource consulting projects and manage projects, including budgets and technical staff. Creatively and aggressively expand the company's client base and revenue. Qualifications: Graduate degree in archaeology, anthropology or history; bachelor's degree with equivalent experience will be considered. Five years of experience in fieldwork and report completion. Must be able to serve as Project Archaeologist or Principal Investigator under the Secretary of the Interior or Texas Antiquities Code guidelines. Experience providing leadership for and management of other professionals.

A national full-service environmental firm is seeking a staff archaeologist/field director to work within an established Cultural

continued

Resources Department. Prehistoric focus preferred. Candidate must meet or exceed the Secretary of the Interior's qualifications, have a working knowledge of the regulatory process, and have demonstrated experience in Phase I, II, and III archaeological fieldwork. Strong technical report writing skills and ability to conduct archival and technical research a must. Travel will be required. M.A. in Anthropology, Archaeology, or other directly related field.

Assistant professor for a tenure-track position. We seek a scholar with a specialization in bio-archaeology or applied forensic anthropology. A Ph.D. is required at time of application.

University seeks nautical archaeologist for an assistant professor tenure-track position. Applicants must have teaching experience in nautical archaeology and artifact conservation methods. In addition to teaching anthropology courses at the undergraduate and graduate levels, responsibilities include supervising the undergraduate Maritime Studies program.

Historic site seeks a curator of archaeological collections, responsible for ongoing laboratory operations, cataloging, curation, and collections research. We seek an individual with experience with relational databases and quantitative computing applications, knowledge of the material culture of the early-modern Atlantic world, and a record of innovative collections-based research.

For jobs with the federal government, go to the website of the Office of Personnel Management at usajobs.opm.gov and search under *archeologist* (the spelling used by the federal government).

Cultural Resources management jobs can be found on the website of the American Cultural Resources Association at acra-crm.org/jobs.html. This site also lists summer jobs for students.

Resources

A number of resources are available to assist you in your job search.

Online Resources

The Princeton Review has information online on archaeology as a career at princetonreview.com/cte.

"Frequently Asked Questions about a Career in Anthropology" are online at museum.state.il.us/ismdepts/anthro/dlcfaq.html.

To learn about archaeology and find links to other archaeology websites, visit cc.ukans.edu/~hoopes/resources.html.

The Cultural Resources section of the National Park service website lists training programs in archaeology, volunteer opportunities, publications, and much more at cr.nps.gov.

The National Trust for Historic Preservation and the National Park Service have produced a series of twenty-two lesson plans called "Teaching with Historic Places," which are available online at cr.nps.gov/nr/twhp/topic .htm#arch.

To stay up-to-date on the latest archaeological discoveries, visit Anthropology in the News, a site that links you to current news stories concerning anthropology and archaeology, at anthropology.tamu.edu/news.htm.

Publications

American Archaeology. A quarterly journal published for members of the Archaeological Conservancy, 5301 Central Ave. NE, Suite 1218, Albuquerque, NM 87108-1517; americanarchaeology.com.

Archaeology. Published bimonthly by the Archaeological Institute of America. Subscription Service, P.O. Box 420423, Palm Coast, FL 32142-0423; archaeology.org.

"Archaeology and You," "The Path to Becoming an Archaeologist," and "Experience Archaeology." Brochures and publications available from the Society for American Archaeology, 900 Second St. NE, #12, Washington, DC 20002-3557; saa.org/publications

Biblical Archaeology Review. Published bimonthly by the Biblical Archaeology Society, 4710 41st St. NW, Washington, DC 20016; bib-arch.org /bswb_BAR/indexBAR.html.

Bulletin of the Society for American Archaeology. An electronic version of past issues of the Society's quarterly bulletin, available at saa.org/publications /saabulletin/index.html.

"Careers in Historical Archaeology." The publication covers historical and underwater archaeology. Available from the Society for Historical Archaeology, 19 Mantua Rd., Mt Royal, NJ 08061; sha.org/sha_cbro.htm.

Common Ground. Published by the National Park Service Archeology and Ethnology Program. Editor, NPS Archeological Assistance Division, P.O. Box 37127, Washington, DC; cr.nps.gov/aad/cg/index.htm.

Current Archaeology. Published bimonthly by Current Archaeology, 9 Nassington Rd., London NW3 2TX, UK; archaeology.co.uk.

Evolutionary Anthropology: Issues, News, and Reviews. Six issues a year from John Wiley & Sons, Subscription Department, 111 River St., Hoboken, NJ 07030; interscience.wiley.com/cgi-bin/jhome/38641.

Historic Preservation. Published bimonthly by the National Trust for Historic Preservation. Membership Department, National Trust for Historic Preservation, 1785 Massachusetts Ave. NW, Washington, DC 20036; nationaltrust.org/magazine/current/index.htm.

KMT: A Modern Journal of Ancient Egypt. A quarterly journal. KMT, Department G, P.O. Box 1475, Sebastopol, CA 95473; egyptology.com/kmt.

Minerva. A British archaeology magazine published bimonthly. Minerva Magazine, 14 Old Bond Street, London W1X 4JL, UK; minervamagazine.com.

Near Eastern Archaeology. A quarterly magazine from American Schools of Oriental Research, Membership/Subscriber Services, P.O. Box 133117, Atlanta, GA 30333; www.asor.org/pubs/index.html.

"Summer Field School List." Compiled by the American Anthropological Association, 2200 Wilson Blvd., Suite 600, Arlington, VA 22201; aaanet.org.

Professional Associations for Archaeology

American Anthropological Association
Archaeology Section
2200 Wilson Blvd., Suite 600
Arlington, VA 22201
aaanet.org

American Cultural Resources Association
6150 East Ponce de Leon Ave.
Stone Mountain, GA 30083
acra-crm.org/index.html

Archaeological Conservancy
5301 Central Ave. NE, Suite 1218
Albuquerque, NM 87108-1517
americanarchaeology.com

Archaeological Institute of America
656 Beacon St.
Boston, MA 02215
archaeological.org

National Trust for Historic Preservation
1785 Massachusetts Ave. NW
Washington, DC 20036
nationaltrust.org

Register of Professional Archaeologists
5024-R Campbell Blvd.
Baltimore, MD 21236
rpanet.org

Society for American Archaeology
900 Second St. NE, #12
Washington, DC 20002-3557
saa.org

Society for Archaeological Sciences
Office of the General Secretary
SAS, Department of Geosciences
Franklin & Marshall College
Lancaster, PA 17604
socarchsci.org

Society for Historical Archaeology
19 Mantua Rd.
Mt. Royal, NJ 08061
sha.org

9

Path 4:
Museums and Libraries

Museums and libraries provide another interesting area of work for many anthropologists.

Museums

There are more than sixteen thousand museums in the United States. About seven hundred are museums of natural history, anthropology, archaeology, or science and technology. Although some anthropologists work in art museums, most find employment in history or natural history museums. The famous anthropologist Margaret Mead worked for decades at the American Museum of Natural History in New York City, for example. Natural history museums are dedicated to research, exhibition, and education in the natural sciences. These museums vary in their size and contents and could include all or some of the following departments: anthropology, astronomy, botany, entomology, fossil and living vertebrates, geology, herpetology and ichthyology, mammalogy, mineralogy, ornithology, and vertebrate paleontology. Collections could include artifacts from ancient civilizations, gems and jewels, fossils, meteorites, and animals from around the world displayed in lifelike settings.

Traditionally, anthropologists working in museums have mainly held the title of curator. In the last two decades, however, more anthropologists have begun taking administrative and other roles.

Definition of the Career Path
The American Association of Museums (AAM) has identified dozens of museum and museum-related career categories. Several of those are exam-

ined here, along with the expected requirements for education, experience, knowledge, abilities, and skills.

Archaeologist. Many natural history museums either have full-time archaeologists on staff or give joint appointments to archaeologists who also have appointments at universities. During the summer months, college students—and sometimes even high school students—are brought on board to help out with summer field programs.

For more information on archaeology as a career, refer to Chapter 8.

Collections Manager. Collections managers supervise, number, catalog, and store the specimens within each division of the museum. In some museums, this position is called registrar.

An undergraduate degree in the area of the museum's specialization is required for this position; an advanced degree in museum studies with a concentration in a specific discipline is recommended. At least three years' experience in a museum registration department or in a position in which the main duties are the technical aspects of handling, storage, preservation, and cataloging is also required.

Prospective collections managers must have knowledge of information management techniques, the ability to accurately identify objects within the museum's collection, and knowledge of security practices and environmental controls.

Conservator. Objects come to museums in varying conditions, and all are subject to ongoing decay. Conservators work to prevent that decay. They help prevent deterioration through a number of steps:

1. *Examination* to determine the object's nature, properties, and method of manufacture, and the causes of deterioration
2. *Scientific analysis and research* to identify methods and materials used to produce the object
3. *Documentation* of the condition of the object before, during, and after treatment, and to record actual treatment methods
4. *Preventive measures* to minimize further damage by providing a controlled environment
5. *Treatment* to stabilize the object or to slow deterioration
6. *Restoration*, if needed, to bring an object closer to its original appearance

A conservator working in a natural history museum will be concerned with a variety of objects and materials. There are jobs in architectural conservation and library and archives conservation as well as museum conservation.

Conservators are highly trained professionals who have gone through a number of steps to gain their expertise. Training programs are few and, as a result, are very competitive.

According to the American Institute for Conservation of Historic and Artistic Works, the qualities a conservator must have are: an appreciation and respect for cultural property of all kinds—their historic and sociological significance, their aesthetic qualities, and the technology of their production; an aptitude for scientific and technical subjects; patience for meticulous and tedious work; good manual dexterity and color vision; the intelligence and sensitivity needed to make sound judgments; and the ability to communicate effectively.

Traditionally, training is gained through a graduate academic program, which takes from two to four years. Apprenticeships or internships are a vital part of training and are usually taken during the final year of study. Some programs offer internships that run concurrently with classes.

During a training program, student conservators work with a variety of materials before specializing in a particular area. They learn skills to prevent the deterioration of paintings, paper and books, fiber, textiles, ceramics, wood, furniture, and other objects.

Admission requirements for the various graduate programs differ. All of the programs require academic prerequisites, including courses in chemistry, art history, studio art, anthropology, and archaeology. Some programs prefer candidates to already have a background in conservation. This experience can be gained through undergraduate apprenticeships and fieldwork in private, regional, or institutional conservation laboratories. A candidate's portfolio must demonstrate manual dexterity as well as familiarity with materials and techniques.

Curator. Curators are specialists in a particular academic discipline relevant to a museum's collections. They are generally responsible for the acquisition, care, and interpretation of all objects and specimens on loan or belonging to an area of the museum, and they are knowledgeable about each object's history and importance. Depending on the museum and its area of interest, curators may work with textiles and costumes, paintings, memorabilia, historic structures, crafts, furniture, coins, or a variety of other historically significant items.

Museum curators also conduct research, publish the results, give public presentations, prepare or supervise the preparation of displays and exhibits, and compile and edit catalogs of museum exhibitions. Increasingly, curators need to be familiar with digital imaging and scanning technology since many are responsible for posting images on the museum's website. Curators often work as part of a team with other department curators, conservators, exhibit designers, educators, and registrars.

Curators normally possess an advanced degree with a concentration in an area related to the museum's collections. Three years' experience in a museum or related educational or research facility is usually required before a candidate can advance to a full curatorial position.

Applicants for curatorial positions must be able to explain and interpret the collection to the public and be familiar with the techniques of selection, evaluation, preservation, and exhibition of the museum's collection.

Development Officer. Because most museums depend on donations, membership fees, and grants for their funding, the development office is a vital organ in any museum. Development officers are responsible for fundraising—for planning and implementing special fund-raising events, conducting membership drives, and pursuing grants and donations.

To qualify for a position as a development officer, the following skills are most important: people skills, organizational skills, and the ability to work as part of a team.

To pull together all the elements of a successful fund-raising campaign, development offices rely heavily on the help of volunteer staff. Thus, experience as a volunteer in this department, as in any other museum department, is a great way to get your foot in the door.

Director. Museum directors must be knowledgeable about the museum's collections and be responsible for acquisitions, preservation, research, and presentation. Director also must be familiar with policy making, raising money, managing budgets, supervising staff, and coordinating museum activities.

An advanced degree in the area of the museum's specialty is required for the position, with course work in museum administration. At least five years or more of management experience in a museum or related institution is usually required. Anthropologists working in other departments may sometimes advance to an administrative role.

Applications for the position of museum director should have specialized knowledge of at least one area of the museum's collections or in the management of the particular type of museum. Their area of expertise must also include implementing policies and financial planning.

Educator. Museum educators enhance public awareness of and access to the museum's collections. Museum educators must be able to translate important concepts into understandable language and to convey the excitement and importance of research. Emphasis is placed on being able to communicate ideas to the public and to the institution's administration, grant agencies, and the news media. To do this, educators design and implement programs encompassing a variety of media and techniques and arrange for special events, workshops, and teacher training programs.

Museum educators often work cooperatively as part of a team and interact with other academics and other kinds of museum professionals, such as artists, model makers, and exhibit designers. In addition, educators might train docents and tour guides and might have other supervisory and administrative duties.

An advanced degree in anthropology, education, museum education, or an area of the museum's specialization is usual required for the postion, as well as two years in a museum education department or other related facility.

Candidates for museum education positions must have the ability to prepare material for publications and exhibitions, skill in oral and written communication, and knowledge of school curricula and of research techniques.

Exhibit Designer. Exhibit designers work closely with curatorial and educational personnel to turn ideas into permanent or temporary exhibits. They use drawings, scale models, special lighting, and other techniques. Exhibit designers may have administrative responsibilities and also may supervise the production of exhibits.

Exhibit personnel usually function as part of a team, which could include any or all of the following professionals: designers, who plan exhibits; cabinetmakers, who build the cases for exhibits; sculptors, who make miniatures and models for exhibits; taxidermists, who mount the skins and hides of animals in lifelike positions for study and display; silk screeners and other artists, who create the labels; scientific illustrators, who provide sketches and detailed drawings of different objects; and computer-aided design (CAD) professionals, who translate the sketches and drawings of proposed designs and exhibits into finished blueprints.

Exhibit personnel usually have strong art backgrounds, including a degree or certification in graphic or industrial design, commercial art or communications arts, architecture, interior design, or studio arts. Experience in exhibition design and related construction work with wood, metal, or plastics is usually also required, as well as a portfolio of past and current work.

Museum Librarian. Most midsize to large museums maintain extensive libraries with collections related to the museum's focus. And just as in any library, a museum library needs a professional staff to carry out operations.

The head librarian, usually assisted by one or more assistant librarians, is responsible for acquiring library materials; maintaining the catalog of publications, reference materials, and periodicals; responding to public inquiries; and providing reference and research materials to museum staff.

Museum librarians go through the same educational preparation as librarians in other public or private facilities. The minimum requirement is usually a master's in library science (M.L.S.).

Tour Guide or Docent. Although most museums rely on volunteers as tour guides and docents (the two job titles have essentially the same meaning), there are still a few spots for a paid professional. Most tour guides have a college degree in either education or the field of study the particular museum encompasses.

Training and Qualifications

With museums offering so many diverse careers, it stands to reason that avenues of training leading to these professions would be equally diverse. An objects conservator would have a background different from a curator; an educator's preparation would differ from an exhibit designer's.

In addition, different museums often look for different qualifications. For some museums, candidates must have an advanced degree or a certificate in museology or museum studies. For others, professionals with strong academic concentrations in, for example, anthropology, art history, or history are hired. A combination of academic and hands-on training earned through internships or volunteer programs make a good impression at most museums.

Training Options. How you prepare for a museum career will depend on your interests and circumstances. If you are clear from the start what avenue you wish to pursue, you can tailor-make a course of study for yourself at the university of your choosing. The courses you'll take or the degree you'll pursue will also depend on whether you are a student new to the field or a museum professional making a midcareer change.

Traditionally, new hires to the field of museum work have completed a bachelor's and master's degree in academic disciplines appropriate to the

intended career. For example, curators for natural history museums have studied biology, anthropology, archaeology, and so on. While such a background still serves as the main foundation for successful museum work, over the last three decades, more people have explored university programs offering practical and theoretical training in the area of museum studies. Courses such as museum management, curatorship, fund-raising, exhibition development, and law and museums offer a more specific approach to the work at hand. This, coupled with a broad background in liberal arts or specialization in an academic discipline, provides the museum professional with a knowledge base better designed to serve the needs of the museum.

Whatever your course of study, these days most museums require a graduate degree, either in an academic discipline or in museum studies, museum science, or museology. Also required is an intensive internship or a record of long-term volunteer work.

Three possible tracks a student can follow to prepare for a career in museums are:

- *Track One:* a bachelor's degree in liberal arts or a specific academic discipline; a master's degree or certificate in museum studies, museology, or museum science; and an internship with a museum in a particular field
- *Track Two:* a bachelor's degree in liberal arts or specific academic discipline; a master's degree or doctorate in a specific academic discipline; and an internship with a museum in a particular field
- *Track Three* (for the museum professional changing careers or upgrading skills): a master's degree or certificate in museum studies or a noncredit-bearing certificate in museum studies (short-term course)

The internship is considered the most crucial practical learning experience and is generally a requirement in all programs. The internship can run from ten weeks to a year, with varying time commitments per week. Many graduate programs require the successful completion of six or more courses in addition to the internship.

Finding a Program. The Smithsonian Institution Center for Education and Museum Studies lists museum training programs at all levels offered by universities at museumstudies.si.edu/traindirect.htm. The Smithsonian's Council on Museum Anthropology lists undergraduate and graduate museum training programs for anthropology students on their website at nmnh.si.edu/cma/survey.html.

The American Association of Museums (AAM) offers a publication called "Graduate Training in Museum Studies: What Students Need to Know." It does not list graduate programs but provides information on choosing between a certificate program or a master's degree and on finding an internship. "Graduate Training in Museum Studies" can be purchased from the AAM bookstore or online at aam-us.org.

Information on becoming a conservator and a listing of training programs in conservation can be found on the website of the American Institute for Conservation of Historic and Artistic Works at aic.stanford.edu. The Smithsonian Institution website has a section on Art Conservation Training: Sources for Degrees, Seminars and Mid-Career Training Programs at si.edu/scmre/takingcare/constrng.htm.

Volunteering and Internships. Although formal, academic training is vital to your résumé, hands-on experience is of equal importance. Not only does it provide a host of significant skills, but it also allows you to make an informed decision about the suitability of museum work. Starting with a term of volunteer work, even before beginning a college program, will give you a better idea of what career options museums have to offer and whether these options are right for you.

Many museums rely heavily on volunteer energy, placing volunteers in almost every museum department, from tour guide and gift-shop sales to assisting curators and exhibit designers. The easiest way to volunteer your time is to call a museum and ask to speak to the volunteer coordinator. He or she will work with you to match your interests with the museum's needs.

Most academic museum studies programs require an internship before a degree or certificate can be awarded. In addition, many museums have their own internship programs for full-time students as well as for recent graduates. You can check with your university department first to see what arrangements they traditionally make. If you must arrange your own internship, either during your academic program or after you've graduated, contact the museum's internship coordinator. If the museum has no formal internship program, talk first to a museum staff member to determine where there might be a need. Then write a proposal incorporating your interests in a department where help will be appreciated.

Internships can be either paid or unpaid and are usually a more formal arrangement than volunteering. The number of hours and weeks involved will be structured, and the intern might be expected to complete a specific project during his or her time there. College credit can often be given. When it comes time to hunt for jobs, a successful internship or stint of volunteer work can open the door at the training institution or at other museums.

The AAM publishes a resource report called "Standards and Guidelines for Museum Internships." It covers what museums expect from their interns and what interns can and should expect from the museum. This report is available through the AAM bookstore at aam-us.org.

Career Outlook

Each year, more historic buildings are nominated for inclusion on the National Register of Historic Places. Many of these sites are operated as historic house museums open to the public, which means that more employment opportunities are opening up for museum workers.

History museums are not the only opportunities expanding across the country. Art galleries and art museums can be found in almost any city; science museums, discovery centers, and planetariums are maintained in most midsize to large cities or university towns.

New job titles have been added to the list that was once limited to curators and librarians. The field of museum work is now open to all sorts of professionals, including conservation specialists, designers, planners, finance and budget managers, information specialists, fund-raisers, and many more.

Although the competition in some sectors is stiff, and museum funding always seems to lag behind public demand, a persistent anthropology graduate can get a leg up through volunteering or participating in a student internship.

Earnings Within Museums

Museum salaries vary widely from position to position. Factors such as the source of funding or the region of the country determine salary levels more than the complexity of the job or the level of the candidate's education and experience.

A tour guide might earn $6 to $10 an hour; an assistant curator in the mid- to high thirties a year; a director, from $50,000 on up. Museum curators with the federal government average $64,600 a year. Museum specialists and technicians in government jobs have median salaries of $44,700.

Close-Ups

The following firsthand accounts from anthropologists show how they are using their degrees and skills in a variety of museum settings.

Jim King—*Museum Director.* Jim King was the director of the Carnegie Museum of Natural History in Pittsburgh from 1987 to 1996 and of the Cleveland Museum of Natural History from 1996 to 2001.

He attended Alma College, a liberal arts college, graduating with a B.A. in biology. He earned a master's degree at the University of New Mexico and a Ph.D. in geology at the University of Arizona in 1972.

He taught at the University of Arizona, then received a National Science Foundation grant with a colleague to do archaeological work on extinct animals. He worked at a museum in Illinois, moving up through the ranks from assistant curator to full curator to chief scientist, then to assistant director for sciences.

"I was responsible for all aspects of the museums I led. I had a board I worked with. We met four times a year and reviewed directions and policies. I implemented those policies.

"I had an inner cabinet of my management committee: the head of the exhibit department, the head of the education department, the assistant director for sciences, and the assistant director for administration. On a typical day, I might wrestle with space issues—getting some modifications done to storage areas, for example—make sure that the air-conditioning work got done, and deal with financial issues or personnel issues. As the director, you're the mediator, the court of last resort. Most of my time was in guiding, leading, helping things happen. I probably spent 20 to 30 percent of my time fund-raising.

"We also tried to cultivate our members. One of the programs museums offer is special travel with a board member or curator to some destination. I've taken a group to Kenya, for big game viewing, and to Antarctica for whale watching and viewing penguins.

"My favorite part of my job was watching some of the world's greatest staff do good things. They were expected to raise grant funds to support their research; to publish; and to have a national, even international, reputation. When a curator got a major paper published in a journal or [got] a new grant for something, that was probably the best part of my job.

"It also pleased me to get letters from people saying things like, 'My son's third-grade class was in your museum, and one of your educators just did a sterling job.' That really made me feel good.

"A museum is a fantastic setting from which to do research. Museums are, as far as I'm concerned, a better location to do this than a university. They have the collections, and second, you're not saddled with teaching duties. A beginning professor always has courses to teach. Here, a beginning curator has a lot more time to work on his or her research.

"To work in a museum, you need to get a good education, a good grounding in whatever chosen area, whether it be teaching, or science, or artistic skills. We had very few 'museum study' people on our staff. Not that we wouldn't hire them, but we found over the years that the majority of new employees came to us with traditional academic backgrounds. Some might go out and take a short course in museum techniques, but most had at least a bachelor's degree in a field that relates to what the museum does, anthropology, or one of the geology areas, say studying fossils.

"Go in and talk to people in the museum. I probably talked to half a dozen people a month who came in through the door and wanted to know about careers in museums. I'd talk to them for a while, and then if they were interested in science, I'd have them spend an hour or two talking to a curator, or they might go and spend time in our education program, just watching.

"And volunteer. Two high school seniors who were interested in careers in anthropology volunteered in our anthropology program during the summer. We gave them the whole range of what a museum anthropologist does."

Joan Gardner—Chief Conservator. Joan Gardner is the former chief conservator at the Carnegie Museum of Natural History in Pittsburgh. She retired in 1999 after twenty years with the museum.

"I had been a science and math teacher and a social worker, then decided to change careers and went back to school as an adult. I was involved in a joint program with George Washington University and the Smithsonian Institution.

"My thesis director took me to the Smithsonian, where they had just developed a program in museum studies with a conservation component. When I walked into the lab, I knew then that that was what I wanted to do. I'd always been fascinated with anthropology, and archaeology in particular. You can't get into this profession without being fascinated with the objects that people produce in various cultures around the world, and what these objects mean, and why they're done the way they are. I was enrolled in a special studies program for my master's (the program is no longer in existence), with an emphasis in conservation. It was split between anthropology and art history, and I had a strong science background. There's an emphasis on chemistry.

"All programs have an internship. I did mine at the Smithsonian during the entire three years. It was almost a full-time job for me, fitting classes in between my hours at the Smithsonian. I got my master's, then came directly to Carnegie.

"As an objects conservator for a natural history museum, I probably saw a wider range of items than your average art museum conservator. I worked with a variety of anthropological objects, including skins, hides, fur, Indian robes, wooden dolls, and feathered headdresses.

"Many of these garments and items were not meant to last longer than a few years, but some of them have now lasted several hundred. A conservator's efforts show long-lasting results.

"We didn't do a lot of restoration work; we tried to keep the object's integrity intact as much as possible. Restoration is often conceived of as trying to bring something back to its condition when it was new. That's not what we were after at all. We wanted to slow down further deterioration. We tried to use only materials that were compatible and that we knew have proved to be reversible or would not cause some sort of contamination of the object.

"I've worked with a Hopi headdress that a child would wear. It was made of wood and painted, with feathers and leather straps. Then we had these huge headdresses from the Plains groups such as the Crow, the Arapaho, and the Lakota. They're made with dyed horse hair and eagle feathers.

"I've also worked on a bentwood box from the Northwest Coast Indian group named Haida. I researched the materials it was made from, how it was made, the colorants. We could take samples and send them off for analysis, or we might use our own microscope to try to determine what the origin of the dye or paint was. The box was badly abraded and broken in many places. So, I didn't touch it until I documented what it looked like, where the breaks were, where modern materials had been used on it. We took photographs of it before we worked on it, during the work, and then after we'd finished, so there's a record for history.

"Pittsburgh has been an industrial city for a hundred years, so here we have a real problem with particulates and soot. In the early days, most objects were displayed on open shelves. They didn't have the great storage cabinetry we have now. One of our biggest jobs was trying to remove the soot without damaging the pigment or diluting it.

"Being a conservator is a real team effort. Very often the curator and I looked under the microscope and discussed what we should do with a piece that's damaged, whether to leave it alone or just make it stable so it wouldn't cause any further loss.

"I also dealt with the exhibits department. I told them how they could build a mount for an object so that the object was supported. They arranged for proper lighting levels so the colors didn't fade. I also worked closely with curators transporting objects. How an object is supported or wrapped so it can go to another museum without damage often falls into the conservator's realm.

"Before you go for your master's degree, you have to demonstrate a good knowledge of chemistry, you have to be good with your hands, and you have to be really bright. Almost every student has some talent, in painting, pottery, working with metals. Most people have a portfolio before they go on for their master's.

"Your master's degree will cover theory as well as practical experience. Usually by the time you're a third-year student, you know what you want to specialize in. If, for example, you know you want to go into textiles, you find a museum and internship in the area of your interest.

"It's a wonderful profession, but you have to be able to deal with things that require an awful lot of patience. My master's work involved unfolding and stabilizing some fabrics that were in a mound, buried in A.D. 1200. They were so dry that they'd shatter in your hands. Frankly, it's not something that most people have the patience for.

"By the time you graduate with your master's, you will be a skilled conservator. But unfortunately, walking into a job in a natural history museum is not a shoo-in. Very often museums send their work to a private conservator because they can't afford to have a full-time conservator on staff.

"A lot of new graduates go into private practice. Although it is expensive for a new graduate to set up a private practice (the lab chemicals alone are very costly), once in practice, an independent conservator can do quite well."

Strategies for Finding the Jobs

Anthropologists can sometimes find employment locally—in a local history or natural history museum, for example. To broaden your opportunities, however, chances are you'll have to relocate. If you have a place in mind where you'd like to work, a phone call or an introductory letter sent with your résumé is a good way to start. The "Resources" section at the end of this chapter also lists several directories that can lead you to interesting destinations.

Because many museums are state or federally operated, you might have to obtain a special application through the state capital or from Washington, D.C. For jobs with the federal government, go to the Office of Personnel Management website at usajobs.opm.gov.

Many professional associations maintain websites with job listings and upcoming internships and fellowships. Addresses of some key organizations are provided at the end of this chapter.

The *Official Museum Directory*, compiled by the AAM, is a valuable resource found in the reference section of most libraries. In addition to its listings of natural history museums, it contains scores of historical and preservation societies, boards, agencies, councils, commissions, foundations, and research industries. You could decide on a region where you'd like to work, then approach your choices with a phone call, résumé and cover letter, or personal visit.

The AAM also publishes a monthly newsletter called "Aviso." At least half of each issue is devoted to listings for employment opportunities and internships. "Aviso Employment Resources Online," a supplement to the newsletter, can be found at aam-us.org. Here are just a few examples of the types of jobs advertised in one issue. Because the positions have already been filled, the names of the hiring body and contact information have been deleted.

A museum of archaeology and anthropology at an eastern university anticipates funding for a nine-month collections management internship. Interns participate in a comprehensive training program and supervise volunteers in storage renovations and computer inventory of a designated collection. Candidate should be interested in a museum career and have a background in archaeology/anthropology or museum studies.

University is seeking a director for its museum. Professional staff appt. Ph.D. in anthropology or related field req'd. Southwestern or Latin Amer specialization. Must have the ability to administer the educational, research, and service activities of an anthropological museum. Museum work will be combined with teaching two courses per year in the dept of Sociology and Anthropology.

State museum seeks energetic, experienced curators for regional branches. Opportunity to develop changing exhibits, organize special events, and create and execute school programs. Duties include development and supervision of a docent program and implementation of community outreach activities. Qualifications include a B.A. in American history, American studies, anthropology, archaeology, art history, historic preservation, museum studies, or fine arts, with a minimum of three years professional curatorial experience (or an M.A. plus one year of experience).

Public museum, a recognized leader in human and natural history, seeks a vice president of education and public programming. Will develop and oversee all aspects of the education and public programming department, including distance learning, fee-based programming, informal education, and teacher training. Requirements: B.A.; master's degree preferred in a related discipline. Teaching certification a plus. Must have five to ten years' related experience or a combination of experience and training. Advanced management and budget skills are also required.

Curatorial Assistant for Collections, Medical Museum. Assists in maintaining the order and special care of collections. Includes specific and in-depth identification of specimens, verification and documentation of collection items, cataloging specimens in the collections database, and assisting in preservation of objects. Qualifications: B.S. or B.A. in Anthropology, specializing in physical, forensic, biological, or medical anthropology. Familiarity with exhibition preparation and appropriate care and handling techniques in keeping with modern museum standards.

Libraries

There are more than 100,000 libraries in the United States. More than 90,000 are in elementary and secondary schools, 9,000 are public libraries, and about 3,600 are libraries in colleges and universities. An additional 9,000 are special libraries in businesses, law firms, museums, and other institutions.

Definition of the Career Path

While we traditionally think of libraries as housing books, newspapers, maps, and journals or periodicals, they collect materials in all formats. Libraries house microforms, sound recordings, and videos or DVDs and provide access to many online resources that are only available by subscription. While school librarians may work alone, performing all library functions themselves, in larger libraries people have specialized jobs. The following positions are found in academic libraries:

A *bibliographer* selects materials in one or more academic disciplines.

An *acquisitions librarian* orders library materials, with a knowledge of which vendors provide the best service and prices.

Catalogers catalog and classify materials that the library acquires.

An *interlibrary loan librarian* borrows materials the library doesn't own from other libraries and reciprocates by lending materials from the library to other libraries that need them.

A *circulation librarian* supervises the circulation of library materials and the maintenance of the book stacks.

An *instructional librarian* instructs students in research procedures and the use of libraries.

A *reference librarian* provides reference services by answering questions for library users in person, over the phone, or via mail or e-mail.

Large libraries may have specialized positions such as government documents librarian, systems librarian, map librarian, area studies librarian (Africana, East Asian, etc.), conservation librarian, or rare books librarian.

Large universities often have branch libraries serving such areas as science and engineering or art.

Training and Qualifications

Most librarians have a master's degree in library science from a university accredited by the American Library Association (ALA). There are about fifty of these accredited schools in the United States. In addition, some library schools now have distance education programs for students who are not able to reside on campus. The ALA's website at ala.org provides more information about graduate degrees and careers in librarianship. The typical master's degree program takes from one calendar year to two years.

Admission to a graduate library school requires an undergraduate degree in a liberal arts subject. People with undergraduate degrees in anthropology can be found working in all kinds of libraries. However, those with a graduate degree in anthropology will find their degree especially useful to them in a college or university library. There they might be a bibliographer for the social sciences, selecting new materials for those disciplines, or work in a specialized collection like African Studies.

Career Outlook

Large numbers of academic librarians are due to retire in the next two decades. However, as universities cut costs, all these librarians may not be replaced. If you are able to move to where the jobs are, you should find many opportunities. Remember that some of our nation's greatest libraries are in places like Bloomington, Indiana, and Champaign, Illinois.

Earnings Within Academic Libraries

The average beginning salary for academic librarians is $35,000. The median salary for librarians in research libraries (those in institutions granting a large number of Ph.D.s) is $52,000. The head of a branch library averages more than $60,000 and directors of large university libraries average more than $130,000.

Close-Up: Gregory Finnegan, Anthropology Librarian

Gregory Finnegan is Associate Librarian for Public Services and Head of Reference, at the Tozzer Library, at Harvard University.

Getting Started. "I graduated with a degree in liberal arts from Raymond College of the University of the Pacific, an experimental college. I had applications in to library school during my senior year, but it was the 1960s and

I was going to save the world through anthropology. I got a Ph.D. in social anthropology from Brandeis University, with field research in Antigua in the West Indies and in what is now Burkina Faso. For seven years I taught in an integrated department of sociology and anthropology at Lake Forest College in Illinois. During this period the college had declining enrollments and most of the faculty were tenured. As a result, I didn't get tenure.

"In 1979, the job market for anthropologists was officially worse, according to Department of Education statistics, than that for English or philosophy professors. I was reluctant to drag a family to temporary fill-in jobs.

"While teaching, I had come to know several of the college librarians and they encouraged me in my alternative plan to go to library school. I chose the University of Chicago (which has since closed its library school) because it was known to have a large percentage of students with advanced degrees and it was easily accessible by public transit.

"Another part of my introduction to librarianship was the Herskovits Library of Africana at Northwestern University, the leading African studies library in the United States. I came to know the staff at the library and enhanced my awareness of research libraries and the role of their staff in assisting scholars.

"Another reason for changing careers was the realization that I enjoyed one-on-one communication with students more than lecturing to a classroom of students. I imagined that this sort of contact would carry over to reference work in academic libraries and it did. There is a truism in reference service that the first question asked is not the user's real question. The relationship between ethnographic interviewing and the reference interview is very close, and the interviewing skills learned in anthropology are essential to reference work.

"The shift from being a professor to being a student again was an interesting one, one that perhaps all professors should be required to undergo. As one who had celebrated his Ph.D. comprehensive exams as 'the last test' it was startling to revert to tests and papers again."

The Realities of the Job. "After graduation, I accepted a job at a Chicago university that served mostly commuting students. I was the circulation and interlibrary-loan librarian. That first job was a significant qualification in my being recruited as head of public services at the world's leading anthropology library at Harvard. Most academic librarians with Ph.D.s wind up as subject-specialist bibliographers, building collections in their area of expertise. Because I'd had experience administering the more mechanical aspects of public service, I was seen as having rare skills for a subject specialist.

"Motivated both by a desire to use my subject skills and a family desire to return to New England, I then became humanities and social sciences reference-bibliographer at Dartmouth College. I did general reference work as well as materials selection in anthropology and sociology. As a specialist librarian I had a much better sense of what is happening across the four sub-fields of the discipline than I had when I was teaching six courses a year in one subfield. I was eventually asked to teach one course a year in the anthropology department at Dartmouth.

"I now work at the Tozzer Library of Harvard University. Tozzer is unusual in being a full-service library devoted to anthropology; besides us, there are only three research libraries devoted to the subject. We support the work of researchers at Harvard's Peabody Museum of Archaeology and Ethnology and in the anthropology department at the university as well as students from throughout Harvard.

"As Associate Librarian for Public Services, I supervise the staff who work at our circulation desk, who provide reserve readings for classes, and who assist with interlibrary loans. As Head of Reference, I work with users to help them identify sources for their research, which includes helping them use our online catalog and online bibliographic resources like "Anthropological Literature," the index to articles in anthropology that we produce at Tozzer. My ability to assist them is enhanced because, as an anthropologist, I understand how research is produced, disseminated, evaluated, and used in anthropology. Because we're a specialized library, I'm usually able to spend more time with students than would be possible in larger and busier general libraries. It's not unusual for me to spend forty-five minutes to an hour helping a student with a complicated topic.

"I also do book selection for the reference collection. A colleague, the Associate Librarian for Technical Services and Collections, selects titles to be acquired for the circulating collection.

"An important part of being a librarian is belonging to professional associations that keep you current with people, resources, and developments in your field. The Anthropology and Sociology Section of the Association of College and Research Libraries, itself a division of the American Library Association, serves this purpose. Recently, a group composed chiefly of librarians established the Scholarly Communications Interest Group within the American Anthropological Association to address 'our' issues.

"Many anthropologists are also members of area studies associations, with a geographic rather than a disciplinary focus. All these associations either have librarian groups within the association or which meet alongside it. The

Africana Librarians Council of the African Studies Association is an example of the former; for the latter, the Middle East Librarians Association meets at the annual meeting of the Middle East Studies Association. There are librarian groups for Latin American and Southeast Asian studies, as well."

Advice from Gregory Finnegan. "First, get a job as a student in a library. This is valuable as a reality check, and library schools often assume you have some on-the-job experience. Second, consider getting a second master's degree, in anthropology or some other discipline. Many research libraries require a subject masters as well as the M.L.S. Even when it's not required, it will help you stand out from the rest of the pool of applicants. There are, by the way, some thirty to thirty-five people in the United States and Canada with both a master's degree in library science and a Ph.D. in anthropology. A couple are librarians who later became anthropologists, but most are anthropologists who became librarians. For some, it's been a clear break— their library work has little or nothing to do with anthropology. Others of us have careers for which both fields are essential."

Strategies for Finding the Jobs

Four periodicals carry the most of the ads for jobs in academic libraries. The most recent ads are often available on the publications' websites.

- *American Libraries* magazine, published by the American Library Association: ala.org
- *College & Research Libraries News*, published by the Association of College & Research Libraries, a division of the ALA: ala.org/ACRLTemplate.cfm?Section=Career_Opportunities
- *Library Journal*: libraryjournal.com
- The *Chronicle of Higher Education*: chronicle.com

Here are some examples of jobs from these publications. Because the jobs are no longer open, the employers are not identified here.

A large state university library is looking for a social sciences bibliographer. The bibliographer oversees development of collections within the broad discipline of the social sciences; oversees the collections budget within this broad area;

---

continued

develops one or more disciplines of the library's social sciences collections; and coordinates the activities of the social sciences subject specialists. The candidate should have experience in the development of collections in a major research library; a master's degree from an ALA-accredited library school; and a bachelor's degree in the social sciences. A master's degree in one of the social sciences and supervisory experience is preferred.

Social Sciences Team Leader at a large public university. The team leader will coordinate and supervise the efforts of team members to fulfill collection development, reference, and instruction assignments within the social sciences. Duties will include budget planning and management. The successful candidate will have an M.L.S. from an ALA-accredited library school or a subject master's in the social sciences plus equivalent related library experience; at least five years experience in an academic library; and demonstrated ability to work closely with faculty in support of their research and instructional needs. A Ph.D. in the social sciences is desirable, along with foreign language capabilities, and experience with building electronic resources collections.

Resources

Advisory Council on Historic Preservation
1100 Pennsylvania Ave. NW
Washington, DC 20004
achp.gov

**American Association for State and
    Local History**
1717 Church St.
Nashville, TN 37203
aaslh.org

American Association of Museums
1575 Eye St. NW, Suite 400
Washington, DC 20005
aam-us.org

The AAM publishes the following three reports:

- "Careers in Museums: A Variety of Vocations" gives a broad overview of professional career opportunities in museums, suggests educational qualifications and experience for specific positions, and provides information on how to obtain internships. It also lists job placement resources.
- "Museums: A Place to Work: Planning Museum Careers" provides descriptions of more than thirty positions in museums and the skills and education needed for each one.
- "Museum Studies Programs: Guide to Evaluation" helps prospective students analyze how well a museum studies program will meet their particular needs.

American Institute for Conservation of Historic and Artistic Works
1717 K St. NW, Suite 200
Washington, DC 20006
aic.stanford.edu

American Library Association
50 East Huron St.
Chicago, IL 60611
ala.org

Anthropology and Sociology Section
Association of College and Research Libraries
American Library Association
50 East Huron St.
Chicago, IL 60611
lib.odu.edu/anss

Archaeological Institute of America
656 Beacon St.
Boston, MA 02215
archaeological.org

Association for Living History, Farm, and Agricultural Museums
8774 Rte. 45 NW
North Bloomfield, OH 44450
alhfam.org

Costume Society of America
55 Edgewater Dr.
P.O. Box 73
Earleville, MD 21919
costumesocietyamerica.com

Council for Museum Anthropology
American Anthropological Association
2200 Wilson Blvd., Suite 600
Arlington, VA 22201
nmnh.si.edu/cma/index.html

Heritage Preservation: The National Institute for Conservation
1625 K St. NW, Suite 700
Washington, DC 20006
heritagepreservation.org

National Register of Historic Places
National Park Service
1201 Eye St. NW, 8th floor
Washington, DC 20005
cr.nps.gov/nr

National Trust for Historic Preservation
1785 Massachusetts Ave. NW
Washington, DC 20036
nationaltrust.org

Society for American Archaeology
900 Second St. NE, Number 12
Washington, DC 20002
saa.org

Society of Architectural Historians
1365 North Astor St.
Chicago, IL 60610
sah.org

Index